The Plains Indians

By the Author

THE BUFFALO
HORSES IN AMERICA
THE PLAINS INDIANS

THE
PLAINS
INDIANS

Francis Haines

Thomas Y. Crowell Company

NEW YORK / ESTABLISHED 1834

Maps by Don Pitcher

Copyright © 1976 by Francis Haines

Designed by Ingrid Beckman

Manufactured in the United States of America

Library of Congress Cataloging in Publication Data
Haines, Francis.
    The Plains Indians.

    1. Indians of North America—Great Plains. I. Title.
E78.C73H34   978′.004′97   75-23259
ISBN 0-690-01031-1

1   2   3   4   5   6   7   8   9   10

To my friend Hutch who nudged me into this.

Contents

Maps

Introduction

IN THE FIRST HALF of the nineteenth century twenty-seven tribes of mounted Indians dominated the Great Plains of North America, leaving no room for intruders. All of these Indians were either nomadic buffalo hunters subsisting almost entirely on the teeming herds, or seminomadic tribes with permanent villages and dependent on their crops for about half their food needs, with the buffalo supplying the other half. Although these tribes were of divers language groups and biological backgrounds, they had developed a common culture that pervaded the whole Plains region and made them appear much more homogeneous than they were.

Each of the seminomadic tribes claimed as its own a large expanse of hunting grounds surrounding its villages while the nomadic tribes each laid claim to all the land on which it hunted and camped over the years. Before the white settlers came to the Plains the tribes sometimes fought over conflicting claims to desirable lands, and when the settlers did come each tribe tried to defend its holdings against the intruders. As the settlers swarmed in the Indians sometimes mounted strong attacks against them and soldiers were sent to protect the intruders. Years of spectacular raids and battles followed, all of them duly reported in the nation's press by correspondents traveling with the troops and by small town editors near the field of action. All of these accounts stressed the spectacular and colorful aspects of the conflicts as well as the villainy of the red men.

Fiction writers soon turned to the colorful and well-publicized Indians for the material for their dime novels, and playwrights used the Indians as important actors in their melodramas. The deep interest of the American public, particularly in the eastern states, in the Great Plains, and the nomadic tribes led William F. (Buffalo Bill) Cody to engage a large troop of authentic Plains Indians together with a band of real cowboys to tour the east in his Wild West show. His success soon brought a host of imitators led by William (Pawnee Bill) Lillie. In all about fifty such shows were organized and toured the cities and towns year after year, bringing their color and action to every corner of the country.

In each show bands of gaily painted warriors in their colorful attire dashed about the arena on their "Indian ponies," making attacks on covered wagons or stagecoaches, always to succumb to the cowboys or cavalrymen who dashed in at the critical moment to shoot down those pesky redskins by the dozen. To heighten the appeal of their shows, the promoters tried to get veteran Indian warriors, survivors of the best-known battles and from the highly publicized tribes, the Dakotas, Cheyennes, and Pawnees. Buffalo Bill, through his friendship with the great Sitting Bull, had that Dakota leader and some of his best warriors on the show for several years.

The showy, glamorous regalia, developed largely by the Dakotas to be worn by the warriors and chiefs on ceremonial occasions, was well suited to the show ring, although it had no place on the battlefield. Designed to be worn by a mounted man, it showed to best advantage when the horse moved at an easy lope. The showy war bonnets, especially those with twin tails, were designed for the dry climate of the arid Plains and were never meant for use in the woodlands, damp climates, or indoors. In the arena a warrior also carried his arms, shields, lances, bows and arrows, and sometimes a carbine. He painted his horse and his face in fancy color patterns that had special meaning for him.

These Indians from the open plains were greatly impressed by the glittering finery of the circus performers they met. From them they borrowed freely any items that might enhance their own costumes. They particularly liked ostrich plumes and other exotic feathers enhanced by brilliant aniline dyes, and the spangles and sequins that sparkled so well in the lights. By 1900 such additions had been adopted by their folks back on the reservations and all the Indian costumes became gaudier as they became less authentic.

These Wild West shows enjoyed a great popularity for about thirty years, gradually giving way to the circuses and the new motion pictures, but the public interest in western Indians remained, stimulated greatly by that magazine found in so many American homes, *The Saturday Evening Post*, a reputable family publication that was welcome in the living rooms of middle-class America where dime novels were banned. The *Post* published many western yarns, both short stories and serials, each year, often one each week for a long period, and had them well illustrated, often in full color, for the western Indian in costume and dashing about on his spirited mount was the inspiration and delight of the artists.

These action pictures, displayed week after week through the years, appealed to the entire family, especially to the youngsters. Even before they learned to read the children could enjoy poring over the western scenes where Indian weapons and regalia were displayed to great advantage. From their early interest grew that great childhood game, "Cowboys and Indians," that flourished throughout the land over several generations. Thus without conscious effort all these children absorbed vivid, lasting impressions of how Indians should look and act.

Then the motion picture industry began producing a steady supply of pictures in western settings, with many of them based on the stories from the *Post*. In time these pictures became known generally as "Westerns" and often featured Plains Indians or used them to supply color and action to pictures primarily about whites. Even today, after more than sixty years of the steady production of Westerns, new ones or remakes of the more popular old ones appear in the movie theaters each year.

Following World War II the burgeoning television industry turned to the vast supply of old Western movies to bolster their programs and to keep the younger set glued to the TV picture tube. Later, when television studios turned to Western shows produced especially for the medium, Indians of all kinds from many different tribes scattered from the Atlantic to the Pacific appeared in the various stories. Usually they were shown as mounted Indians in Plains costumes even when the action took place hundreds of miles away from the Plains and the Indians thus depicted were supposedly from tribes that had never been near the Plains and had never worn any such regalia. Hence, most Americans living today have been subjected since early childhood to a steady diet of the culture, habits, and fighting qualities of the Plains tribes.

Such a detailed presentation year after year, decade after decade, of this same short period of Indian culture, spanning the period from 1830 to 1880, has given the Americans in general the concept that these Indians lived in a static society for several centuries. Although the Indians in the stories and shows appear in a great variety of wild episodes, and supposedly are from many different tribes inhabiting many different areas, they always wear the same kind of costumes and behave in the same manner. They are also cast from the same group of "extras" around the movie studios who look like real Indians to the casting directors. Several good, authentic, full-blooded Indians from the Columbia Basin have been refused employment as Indians in shows dealing with their tribe because they did not look like the stereotype Indian extra to the casting director, but since they were good riders and were readily available, they were cast as United States cavalrymen and used in battle scenes to subdue bands of their own people.

The American tourist coming to the western states also carries a vivid impression of how an Indian should look and dress, an impression received directly from the movies, the television shows, and the pictures drawn by the many magazine illustrators. Indians at fairs and exhibitions, demonstrating some of the old tribal skills in authentic surroundings, are expected by these tourists to wear the "real" Indian costume, that of the Plains. Hence a Navaho woman perched on a canyon rim with her genuine old-type loom weaving a Navaho blanket in the customary manner attracted many more tourists and earned more and larger fees for posing for snapshots by wearing a gaudy, modernized Sioux war bonnet, an article that no woman would have been allowed to touch in the old days, a kind of headdress never seen among the Navahos until recent times.

This common, erroneous concept, that all the Plains tribes, and several other tribes on both sides of the Plains, all lived in the same environment, all looked alike, all dressed alike, and all followed the same customs over endless years has led to a serious misunderstanding of the real Indians of the Plains. To further confuse the picture, much of the material presented in both the movies and the TV shows is misleading or downright false. Even trained historians tend to accept without critical evaluation the Indian culture pattern that they absorbed as children through these popular sources since they all seemed to agree on most details.

Evidently, a reexamination and a reevaluation of the whole area of the history and culture of the Plains tribes is now in order, especially since now there is a significant body of newly discovered information on both the earlier years and the various migrations. A general view of this new material, with special emphasis on the migrations, comprises the contents of this book.

First, an attempt will be made to follow the various tribes classed as Plains Indians in the nineteenth century from their earliest recorded appearances until they were finally penned on the reservations toward the close of the nineteenth century. In this way it may be possible to determine when and under what circumstances each of the various tribes reached the buffalo country and took possession of the areas they claimed as their own at the peak of their power. Then an attempt will be made to chart the growth and spread of the general Plains culture that gave all the buffalo-hunting tribes a somewhat uniform appearance by the midnineteenth century and attracted a great deal of interest throughout the civilized world.

Until the present century anthropologists believed that all the Indian tribes in the New World had come from Asia in several migrations during the last few thousand years and that the Great Plains had been entirely empty of humans until about three thousand years ago. Then they believed that a few tribes had moved to the edge of the Plains where they remained until the eighteenth century, and when the Indians finally secured horses from the Spanish who came up from Mexico, they all rushed into the buffalo country and in a short time had taken over the entire area of the Great Plains. However, later research proved that the Plains had been continuously occupied by various hunting bands over a period of several thousand years and their residue in the form of stone tools and weapons, hunting camps, cave shelters, buffalo jumps, and the like were scattered over the entire expanse of the great grasslands. Even though the total number of hunters at any one time was small, possibly never exceeding ten thousand in all, in the course of several thousand years they left identifiable artifacts in hundreds of places, indisputable evidence that they had at one time or another hunted over the whole buffalo country.

When the first Spanish explorers reached the Plains in the sixteenth century and found buffalo-hunting Indians there they assumed that those same tribes had been on the Plains for centuries. Then when these Spanish observers were followed about a century later by other travelers from both Spain and France, and these were followed in turn by traders and trappers, and all of these found Indians scattered over the entire Plains area, it appeared that the Plains had been occupied by many different tribes for several centuries.

The archaeologists and anthropologists then assumed that the tribes present on the Plains and adjacent to them in the eighteenth century were descendants of those older hunters who had left so many traces on the land, and that the Plains had indeed been inhabited for a long time, possibly for about fifteen thousand years. Our concern now is to find out how well the present body of knowledge concerning the Plains and the tribes present there in the nineteenth century supports this assumption.

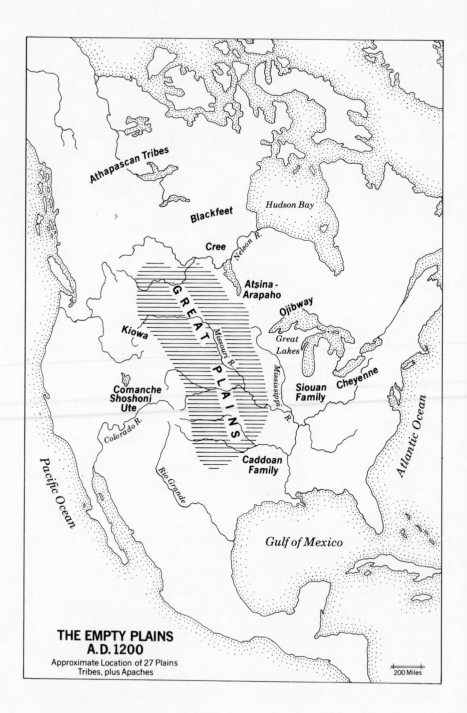

Athapascan Tribes

Blackfeet

Cree

Nelson R.

Hudson Bay

Atsina -
Arapaho

Ojibway

Kiowa

G R E A T

Missouri R.

*Great
Lakes*

Comanche
Shoshoni
Ute

P L A I N S

Mississippi R.

Siouan
Family

Cheyenne

Colorado R.

Atlantic Ocean

Pacific Ocean

Rio Grande

Caddoan
Family

Gulf of Mexico

**THE EMPTY PLAINS
A.D. 1200**

Approximate Location of 27 Plains
Tribes, plus Apaches

200 Miles

1

The Great Plains

THE GREAT PLAINS of North America include most of the heartland of the continent, a vast sea of grass that reaches from central Texas northward into Canada, and from the Rocky Mountains eastward to the forest fringe near the Mississippi River, about a half-billion acres in all. While there is general agreement among the geographers about the boundaries of the central portion, the High Plains, the extreme borders of the Great Plains are poorly defined, especially to the east where the grasslands gradually merge into open woodlands. In the following discussion the Great Plains are considered to be all the open grasslands where the buffalo roamed freely. Here for many thousands of years many kinds of large grass eaters fed in profusion, and here, for forty thousand years or more, small bands of roving hunters preyed on the herds.

During the last ice age, the great ice sheets covering parts of North America and Europe stored so much moisture that the ocean level around the world was lowered about four hundred feet, uncovering what is now the bottom of the Bering Sea and exposing a land bridge between Alaska and Asia over which many kinds of animals passed freely back and forth between the two continents for a few hundred thousand years. Forty thousand years or more ago, when the climate in Alaska and eastern Siberia was moderate and the vegetation on the land bridge grew profusely, herds of grass eaters moved eastward into Alaska and on into the Great Plains along the ice-free corridor between the Rocky Mountains and the Wisconsin ice sheet. Small bands of hunters followed the herds, living well off their kills, not knowing and not caring that they were entering lands where men had never been. On they went following the herds, trending ever southward until their leaders came to the Gulf Coast of Texas. Here the herds of game stopped. They could not move on to the east—for the way was blocked by a wide belt of swamps and the broad Mississippi River. To the west the land was rough and broken, both higher and drier than the grazing animals liked. Hence the hunters stayed in eastern Texas with their favorite game animals, mammoths, giant sloths, and huge prehistoric bison all feasting on the lush vegetation of these warm, moist lowlands.

These hunters still followed the herds in their wanderings, but most of the herds just wandered about in the same large area, no longer interested in striking out for new lands. Here in eastern Texas in the course of time some of the hunters settled in small villages. They found it convenient to store some of their gathered foodstuffs, such as nuts, that were used to supplement their meat diet if hunting failed for a time. To forestall such lean periods, the hunters gathered nuts, bulbs, and roots and put them by for the winter months when any vegetable foods were scarce and hard to find. Such food storage often required the erection of small shelters that also could offer the people some protection from the winter storms. There they could huddle in some comfort, warming themselves by their little fires on the open hearths.

Fortunately for us, the remains of one of their early sites has been uncovered near Lewisville, Texas.[1] There in 1956 workers excavated a cluster of twenty-one hearths, each with an abundance of charcoal. The whole site was surrounded by piles of bones from the various animals that had supplied the meat for many dinners over a long period.

The charcoal was in sufficient quantity at each hearth that good samples could be taken several feet apart and could thus serve as checks for each other by carbon 14 dating. These repeated tests, all done by the most highly trained men in a laboratory with the latest sophisticated equipment and methods, all confirmed that the carbon samples were more than thirty-seven thousand years old, but since that date is near the end of the possible carbon 14 readings, it could not be established any more accurately. It might easily be several thousand years older, but could not possibly be any less. This primitive little village of the ice age in eastern Texas has thus been established as the oldest dated site of man's occupancy in the New World, and adds many thousand years to the proven period of man's arrival in North America. Certainly the hunter ancestors of these Texas people required a long period of time to move down from Alaska and then develop their village culture with well-made hearths. As long as they remained migrating hunters they would have no need to develop such structures.

In the favorable environment of east Texas these ice age villagers multiplied during the succeeding ages and in a period of twenty-five thousand years or more their descendants had spread over the continent of North America wherever it was not covered by the glaciers, but always there were bands of hunters left in the southern grasslands who did not become villagers but continued in their customary pattern as nomadic hunters following the herds, especially the mammoths, although they also killed other large grass eaters that found both the vegetation and the climate to their liking.

A great many of the bones from the dining places of these early hunters have remained to be found by modern excavators. It may be that the large bones of the mammoth were more durable than those of other animals, but it is indicated too that the hunters preferred mammoths both to kill and eat. Camps near the spots of their kills are rich in bones, as are some of the bogs. While bones near the camp have been cut apart from the skeleton and have been moved about, bones in the bogs still remain attached to the skeleton, showing that the flesh had been stripped from the entrapped animal by the hunters who found the unfortunate beast mired down, and who may even have stampeded their giant victim to its death.

Later as the ice sheets around Hudson's Bay melted, the climate of the Plains changed. For a few thousand years the southern plains had been well supplied with moisture by the dependable heavy rains. Streams ran in the valleys, lakes and swamps bordered by wide belts of lush vegetation were scattered profusely over the landscape. Here in the rich pastures the hunters found their choicest game, large, slow animals that could be killed by a small band of hunters and with each carcass furnishing enough meat to feed both the hunters and their families for several days.

After the ice sheets to the north had vanished, the climate became much warmer and drier. As the rainfall diminished, the rivers shrank, many of the swamps and lakes dried up completely, and groves of trees disappeared, while the short grass spread farther and farther across the land. According to some authorities, the enlargement of the grasslands was aided considerably by the recurring grass fires steadily eating away at the fringing woods. Many of these fires were set by lightning, others were man made, either accidentally by untended camp fires or purposely to help drive game to destruction.

As the ice sheet retreated to the north, the grass spread to all the areas uncovered by the melting ice until finally the Plains became a great pasture of some 750,000 square miles that in historic times furnished rich grazing for about thirty million buffalo and two or three million antelope, elk, and deer—in truth, a hunter's paradise.

For some unknown reason, as the pasture lands increased many species of grazing animals died out, especially the largest grass eaters, the mammoth, the giant sloth, and several species of large bison. It may be that these large animals could not thrive on the short grasses of the High Plains, for it would take them too long to secure a sufficient volume of forage. Also such animals might have been seriously handicapped in any environment where they had to range so far from water. Then as the Plains became more arid and the lush growth along the streams decreased, these animals probably moved on to the east, following the streams to a lower elevation where rainfall was more plentiful, but as they moved along they were being gradually crowded into smaller and smaller areas. At the same time the hunting bands and the predators dependent on these animals for their food supply would follow the migrating bands and they too would be concentrated in a smaller area, bringing increased hunting pressure on the herds. Over a period of a few centuries this could result in the gradual extinction of some of the species.

Another development might be expected under these circumstances. As the larger animals became scarcer the hunting bands now living in the open woodlands had to depend more and more on the vegetable foods they could gather. In time such food-gathering activities could lead them to gardening and finally to farming.

While this hypothesis might help explain the dying out of several of the species, and the gradual movement of the hunting bands from the Plains to the woodlands, it is of no help at all with the problem of the disappearance of the smaller grass eaters such as the camel, and especially of the horse, for in historic times feral horses found both the Plains and the western mountain valleys highly suitable to their needs.

The great spaces left vacant by the disappearance of all these species and the new grasslands added around the borders of the Plains were filled in time by herds of bison of a smaller species more adapted to the short grass and the arid climate of the High Plains. These bison came north from Mexico, being gradually pushed out by climatic changes that turned much of northern Mexico from grasslands to desert scrub. The ability of these bison to make the gradual adjustment from their former pastures to the more arid climate of the Plains conditioned these newcomers to survive and prosper in their new environment. Later they proved that they could also adjust to quite a variety of range conditions and of climate as long as there was ample grazing for the herds.

These bison from Mexico made up the great herds that ranged the Plains until the close of the nineteenth century. They usually ranged in herds, each herd being made up of numerous smaller bands of fifteen to fifty animals grazing within a few yards of each other, and all following a commonly recognized leader, usually a wise old cow. As the bison multiplied in their new pastures they spread out in all directions wherever they could find forage and in time covered the land eastward to the tidewater country of Virginia and westward through the mountain passes in the Rocky Mountains into the upper Snake River drainage and the upper watershed of the Colorado River. They were still increasing in numbers and were spreading to new areas, especially east of the Mississippi River, until their further advance was checked by the coming of the white man with horses and guns.

When the bison came to the Plains, with different feeding habits and different ranges than the large grass eaters of the earlier period, some of the small hunting bands followed the new herds, changing their own hunting patterns to adjust to the new game and the new climatic conditions, but when they are said to have followed the herds, they should not be visualized as moving along a mile or two behind the feeding bands, killing an animal every day or so to supply their food. It was impossible for people on foot to keep up with such a herd for more than a day or so. Often the herd moved across a wide stretch of waterless Plain unsuitable for the hunters on foot. Also, once the first kill was made in a band, the whole herd often moved several miles away. So instead of following closely on the trail of the herd, the hunters chose an area where the buffalo were accustomed to feed at certain times of the year.

There in some little draw or thicket near a water supply the hunters camped in hopes that some of the grazing animals would drift close enough to be ambushed. They found their best lurking places near the trails leading down to water. With some luck the hunters could hope to kill several animals, one or two each day, along the different paths before the herd drifted away to new feeding grounds or galloped off in alarm to some distant range, stirred into headlong flight by who knows what trivial matter.

In visualizing the activities of these hunters, keep firmly in mind that the open Plains were awesome to primitive man, vast open expanses beset with many real dangers impelled by forces beyond his comprehension. On bright, sultry days the mighty Thunderbird (god of the storms) brought in great cumulus clouds, their billowing masses towering miles above the Plains, their dark undersurfaces rent by the dread flashing thunderbolts that could strike and kill the unwary man caught in the open with no place to hide. At such times the open Plains were no place for a mere man, helpless beneath the wrath of malevolent spirits with their deadly weapons that flashed and rumbled through the skies.

When the black clouds swept by without releasing any rain, the lightning flashes could set the dry prairie grasses ablaze and woe to any poor people caught in the path of the wind-driven inferno. Or the blue-black clouds might send down gusts of hailstones that seldom killed but were always painful to endure, and such storms left the grass cold and wet for hours, unfit for camping, while the grasslands' fuel, the buffalo chips, were sodden and useless.

Another real danger from a sudden storm was that it might stampede a buffalo herd that could come charging out of the driving rain and hail and trample an entire band underfoot before any danger could be sensed. Also the dark, whirling spouts of tornadoes spread death and destruction across the land, and in the winter arctic storms could come speeding in from the north as a dirty gray front of driving snow and subzero cold. These blizzards could bring death in a short time to the unwary human caught out on the open Plain.

To survive over the years on the High Plains the little hunting bands had to stay within a few miles of some kind of shelter, such as a small cave or a nook beneath a jutting rock ledge, a shrubbery thicket in a draw, a grove of trees or a belt of timber along a watercourse. They could range over the hills for game, but they never dared travel freely across the bare lands at any distance from the shelters needed to protect them from the fierce storm gods.

The autumn months, when nuts, seeds, bulbs, and roots could be harvested, were also the period of the fall hunt when buffalo meat was usually plentiful. From this abundance the people needed to store the least perishable of these foods against the starving times of winter when deep snows and northern storms hindered the hunters. They built small caches for their little hoards near the caves under the rimrock or they built small earth-covered lodges in sheltered spots near the streams and placed their caches close by. The stream usually had some timber along its banks that supplied logs for the lodges and wood for the fires. Once they had developed such a spot they returned to it each winter and over the years some of them learned to do a little gardening, digging up small plots near the winter shelters.

As the climatic changes brought accompanying changes in the variety and distribution of the game animals, the hunters were forced to adapt their hunting methods to meet the new situation. Change came too for the hunters who did not stay on the Plains and learn to live off the buffalo. Even though they followed the mammoths and the other large grass eaters to the east and finally into the forest fringes, they found it increasingly difficult to kill enough of the dwindling herds to meet their needs. The hunters were forced to depend more and more on vegetable foods they could gather. In their new, warmer environment with adequate rainfall they could find some food to harvest for about nine months of the year—bulbs, roots, tender shoots, berries, fruit, and nuts. Over a period of centuries they finally developed into gardeners and settled in villages.

Out on the Plains even the hardiest of the nomadic bands found it tougher to make a living as the drought cut further and further into the shrinking water supply. They moved slowly down the larger streams as the springs and smaller streams failed. Eventually they, too, reached the shelter of the more friendly woodlands and the Plains lay empty and bare of all humans.

There is no solid evidence yet to indicate the approximate time when the last of the hunters moved out, so there is no estimate of how long the Plains were uninhabited, but there is strong evidence to show that in A.D. 1200 there were no Indians anywhere on the Great Plains.

2

The Coming of the Tribes

EVEN DURING THE PERIOD when the hunting bands on the Plains were most numerous, they probably never contained more than ten thousand people in all. They might have been divided into as many as two or three hundred separate bands scattered over most of the Plains area, although they must have lived for the most part along the streams where the larger game animals could be found. Each band probably contained from twelve to fifteen hunters, seemingly the optimum number for the Plains type of hunting as practiced by similar bands in historic times. Out of this total of three hundred bands it is possible that a few of the prehistoric hunters might have remained hidden in some obscure corners of the 750,000 square miles, yet the new tribes coming into the area after A.D. 1200 had no traditions of having to conquer or to displace earlier groups on their arrival, nor do the new tribes in historic times show any alien strains or fragments of language or culture indicating that any such groups had been assimilated.

But such an area as the Great Plains could not remain empty of men for very long when many tribes were living in the regions all around its borders. Once the great drought ended, living conditions along the rivers flowing through the Plains improved rapidly. The rains came again and the land blossomed. Seemingly, the population of the

Caddoan villages in east Texas increased rapidly at the same time until the villages were crowding one another for living room. Under such conditions some fighting must have occurred and the weaker tribes on the fringes of the settlements were pushed from their holdings. When they were finally forced to leave they sought new country either across the Mississippi River to the east or on up the rivers to the northwest where there were no people, good land could be found along the streams, and game was plentiful.

The final impetus might well have been given by the great drought of the thirteenth century. As conditions among the Caddoans worsened rapidly under the impact of this disaster that covered the entire Southwest, the people reached the breaking point. Cornfields withered under the blazing sun and hot, dry winds from the southwest shriveled the half-grown corn in the ear. The food reserves for the winter shrank while hunger pangs increased, furnishing the impelling motive for a large group to move onward in search of a better, less crowded area.

How else can we explain the movement of the Pawnees? When they moved away from their old homes they did not just go to the nearest empty lands suitable for farming. They went north 350 miles or more to the western side of the Missouri Valley in northeastern Kansas and southeastern Nebraska. What made this area of good farming land more desirable than equally good land farther to the south? It easily might have been the presence of large herds of buffalo feeding on the Plains just to the west, an area where they had ranged undisturbed by hunters for countless years. Any Pawnee scouts sent in advance to seek an adequate new homeland could be commended for finding such a suitable place.

The whole tribe then packed up and trekked across the open plains to their new home hindered only by the distance and the summer storms. Since the Pawnees could rather easily complete their entire journey north in about a month, and there is a lack of any positive evidence that they sojourned along the way, it seems probable that the Pawnees moved in one or two large migrations, each taking no more than a month.

Although in historic times the Pawnees still retained a tradition of having moved up from the south, they remembered nothing about finding any other people along the way or in the area where they finally settled, nor did they have any accounts of any fighting with any neighbors during the early period in their new home. From this lack of any information on the subject it would appear that in the early thirteenth century the whole Missouri River Valley was vacant from the mouth of the Kansas River on to the north, although there were populous villages all along the Mississippi River during this same period.

The new environment was somewhat drier than their southern home, but the climate was similar enough that the same methods of farming could be used, and the same crops could be raised. Along the streams flowing into the Missouri River they found enough timber to allow the construction of the same type of houses they had used in the south, but it is probable that they soon substituted earth covering for the lodges for the more open matting more suitable for the warmer clime. The winter storms, with blizzards blowing down from Canada, would soon show them the desirability of having more protection against the cold.

At first in the new land, when their numbers were small, they built a few large villages along the banks of the larger streams, but as their numbers grew, and they spread out to the west, they built many smaller villages, spreading on through the uninhabited country until they finally reached the foothills of the Rocky Mountains near Denver. This period of growth took about three centuries.

The Pawnees were essentially horticulturists, cultivating a large number of small garden plots rather than farming large fields. A very good reason for this was that they lacked the tools necessary to break up the heavy prairie sod on the rich grasslands so they concentrated their efforts on the sandy alluvial fans where their hoes, made from the shoulder blades of buffalo and elk, and their digging sticks were adequate equipment.

They raised good crops of corn, squash, beans, and sunflowers. In addition, they could have for the gathering wild turnips, ground beans, wild plums, wild grapes, several kinds of berries, chokecherries, and some nuts. All of their crops and their gatherings of grain, fruit, and vegetables of various kinds supplied at least one-half of their total food needs. The rest of their food was meat that they secured mostly from the buffalo herds, but they also hunted elk, antelope, deer, rabbits, waterfowl, and game birds.

Even in their small villages the Pawnees built large lodges with heavy wooden frames and strong rafters of timber. These they covered with a heavy layer of grass and over it all they spread a thick layer of dirt. Each of these lodges sheltered about forty people and four or five lodges were adequate for the usual small village. In the larger villages there might be ten or fifteen such lodges scattered about. Such a lodge would last about eight to ten years before the timbers weakened with age and began to sag. It furnished a good shelter both against the summer heat and the bitter cold when the arctic blizzards swept in from the north. The grass layer was useful both in providing the necessary insulation and in keeping the earth from the timbers and so delay their rotting.

When such lodges collapsed from old age it was often more advantageous to build the new ones on some other site where there were trees to supply the timber for building and the wood for the cooking fires. Usually all the timber near the village had become exhausted in the course of ten years and it was simpler and less work to move the people to the new site rather than to transport the large, heavy logs needed for the framework of the new lodges. Of course by the time the old lodge was ready to collapse the village site had accumulated quite a mass of trash and filth, but there is no way of knowing how much such piles were considered as undesirable by the Indians.

The year's activities of the Pawnees were scheduled around their two chief methods of procuring food—growing corn and hunting buffalo. Each spring plots for the corn planting were dug up, with about an acre of land being allowed for each four persons to be fed. With their primitive tools and lack of fertilizer the Pawnees' yield in bushels per acre was rather low. In early May "when the oak leaf is as large as a squirrel's ear" as the old formula goes, the corn was planted. This always put the corn in the ground when the soil was ready whether the season was early or late that year. The young corn needed some care for about a month after the shoots appeared above the ground. During this period it was weeded, and was protected against the raids of rabbits and gophers. Even the deer wandered in at times to nibble at the new growth if they were not deterred.

In about a month the corn stocks toughened and became less attractive to the animals. Then the villagers turned out with their small packs of camping gear. Unlike the nomadic hunters, they did not need to carry along everything they owned, but took only the necessities for a short stay. They then walked out for two or three days into the buffalo country where they broke up into small bands with about twenty-five people in each, seemingly the optimum number for a hunting band in a country well stocked with large game. Only a few people remained behind in the village. They were the very old, the crippled, and some of the smaller children. Thus the hunting band consisted of able-bodied people who could carry packs for several miles a day.

On this early summer hunt the people liked best to kill the young bulls then in prime condition from feasting on the new grass. The cows at this period were not very good for food. They were poor and worn from their spring calving and their coats were all bedraggled. So when the hunters lay in ambush for the buffalo to go to water, they tried to kill one or two of the young bulls, or perhaps a yearling heifer for the camp meat. One of these animals would supply the whole camp for a day or so. As they camped they waited for a small band of buffalo to graze into the proper place where they could be stampeded over a rimrock, a cutbank, or into a swamp.

In such a drive all the buffalo were killed, old bulls, little calves, poor cows, and the desirable young stock. Even the poor meat was rescued and cut into strips for drying and the poorer skins were processed into rawhide while the better skins had the hair removed and were tanned into leather. Cowhides taken at this time were ideal for tipi covers and for some of the heavier clothing and moccasins. The calf skins were thin and light, well suited for clothing and for small bags.

Often such a drive resulted in the destruction of several hundred animals, their mangled bodies piled high at the foot of the buffalo jump. Then the hunters would invite all the other camps within reach to join in the butchery of the game. Even so only a small portion of the carcasses could be used. All the rest remained in a great heap, furnishing food for scavengers as it slowly decayed under the summer sun.

After a month or so of hunting the villagers trudged back, heavily laden with dried meat and hides. If they had been very successful they might have to carry their burdens in relays, each person depositing his load at the new campsite, then returning to the old camp for another load. In addition to the human packers, all the dogs had to help carry loads or to drag them on small travois made by lashing together the small poles used to support the skin tipis which were about six feet high. The larger tipis, so closely associated with the Plains Indians of the nineteenth century, did not come into use until horses were available to transport the heavier skin coverings that the large tipis required.

Back at the home villages the Pawnees busied themselves at processing the skins and with harvesting the first corn of the season that by then was in the milk stage. This green corn could be picked early in August and usually was roasted or boiled in the husk. Then the grains were removed and dried in the sun before being stored for winter. Of course the villagers also feasted on the green corn, and in some years of scant crops the hungry people sometimes left very little corn to store for the winter.

The rest of the corn was left to ripen and was harvested about the middle of September. Then it was shucked, dried, shelled, and put into storage pits. The best ears were selected with care and were put aside to supply the seed corn for the next crop. This seed corn was left on the cob.

With the corn crop safely stored away in the underground pits, the whole village again went out to the buffalo herds for the great fall hunt that lasted for several weeks. By mid-October the buffalo were in prime condition and had grown their new winter coats. Their meat was at its best and the hides were just right to be tanned with the hair on for soft, warm robes. A truly successful hunt required two or three small drives, rather than one big slaughter where many of the hides and much of the meat were wasted before they could be processed. After a small drive the animals were left in better condition and could be cared for properly and promptly. Also, with two or three small drives the camp could feast for weeks on the fresh meat.

In addition to the buffalo hunts the Pawnees liked to stage at least one large antelope drive each year. For this the entire tribe went out to the antelope range and under favorable circumstances might surround several hundred of the animals at one time. The encircling ring of humans was large, so the frightened animals might be chased along the perimeter and would not dash directly across the circle where they would be charging headlong at a thin line of people and could easily break through to their freedom.

As the antelopes tired and slowed their pace, the circle was gradually drawn closer until the totally exhausted animals were strewn about in a small area where they could be dispatched with lances or clubs. Even though one kill might total several hundred antelopes the meat thus secured was much less than that of one successful buffalo drive; for one mature buffalo furnished ten times the amount of meat as was supplied by one antelope. But the antelope was highly prized for its thin, pliable skin which was much better material for many articles of clothing than even the best buffalo hides.

Many elk and some deer were killed throughout the year among the groves and thickets that fringed the watercourses. Their hides too were of great value, for the small antelope hides were insufficient to make dresses for women and hunting shirts for men, each garment requiring the hides of two young elk, preferably two years old. Note that all these hides from young buffalo, antelope, elk, and deer were generally called buckskin by the whites, even though bucks actually furnished only a small fraction of the skins. The finished leather from all of these hides was usually tanned and then smoked, although sometimes skins might be left unsmoked to give a fine white leather.

This rather detailed description of the activities of the Pawnees is given because all the other seminomadic Plains tribes adopted much the same pattern once they became buffalo hunters. This is a strong indication that the presence of buffalo near farming villages tended to produce quite a body of common culture among tribes that had no direct contact with each other.

The migrations of the Pawnees, and some migrations to the east, removed the population pressure among the Caddoan tribes for possibly a century. When the situation again became critical in the fourteenth century the Wichitas were pushed out to the north. They were closely related to the Pawnees and were sometimes called the Black Pawnees, but these two were not considered as two divisions of the same tribe. Even though the two were closely related in language and seemingly were quite friendly, the Wichitas made no attempt to follow the Pawnees and settle near them. Instead they chose a new home site over two hundred miles away from the Pawnee villages.

The propensity of the young men of the Wichita tribe to go roving through new lands was quite evident in the sixteenth century, so it is plausible to assume that when the Wichitas were looking for a new place to settle in the fourteenth century the tribal leaders sent out several of their young men to scout the surrounding country for a good place. Just as the Pawnees had done, the Wichita scouts found an uninhabited area where there were many alluvial fans suitable for garden patches, some trees along the larger streams to supply large timbers for the lodges and fuel for the fires. In addition, the new location was in well-stocked buffalo country.

All of these desirable features the scouts found on the Arkansas River in Kansas, from Great Bend on downstream for about fifty miles. The Wichitas moved out, probably in one large migration, and built many villages on the new land. Their lodges were much like the Pawnee lodges in shape and size, with supporting frames of heavy timbers, but instead of covering their structures with an outer layer of earth, the Wichitas merely used a heavy coat of thatching made from the long reeds and grasses from the moist lands near the river.

The Wichita pattern of living followed closely that of the Pawnees. This was the result of the two tribes living in a similar environment and raising the same crops, rather than any actual copying, for the two were separated by too great an expanse of untraveled Plains to have achieved any significant exchange of culture items, and in their new homes each had to adjust to conditions differing from those they had known in their old homes in the south. The Wichitas raised crops, chiefly corn in their garden patches and stored their surplus for winter in storage pits. They went into the Plains on two large buffalo hunts, one in June and one in the fall, and hunted elk, antelope, deer, and rabbit. Their supply of game birds and waterfowl was less abundant than that of the Pawnees.

It is evident that the Wichita scouts roamed far and wide across the Plains in all directions from their new home. In a few years they had traveled as far as the Pueblo villages along the Pecos River in New Mexico and had made friends with the Pueblo people. From the time of this first contact until hostile tribes moved in and occupied the land to the west of Great Bend, sometime after 1600, the Wichitas made visits to the Pueblos, but probably not as a regular pattern of a visit each year, and whatever trading was conducted between these two groups must have been scanty indeed. Fragments of typical New Mexican pottery have been found in the debris of the old Wichita village sites along the Arkansas River, showing that at least a few of these vessels had been carried more than five hundred miles across the Plains, but the Wichitas did not borrow the Pueblo type of pottery making nor did they copy the Pueblo art of spinning and weaving fibers into cloth. There is no indication that any of the Pueblo Indians ever visited the Wichita villages.

After the Wichitas had been in their new land about two centuries, they were visited by Europeans, the first of the tribes later known as Plains Indians to receive such attention. It was in 1541 that Francisco Coronado finally came to their land that he knew as Quivira. Coronado had come up from Mexico into New Mexico where he left most of his party before he set out to the northeast in search of the fabulous golden cities that he had heard of from the Pueblo Indians and from two Wichitas who were living in New Mexico at the time. He took the two as guides and they led him a merry chase through the new lands as the two of them disagreed on the right way to go. On the return journey Coronado had the services of six new guides from the Wichita villages. These men knew the best route between the two settlements and led him directly back to his destination. It is evident from Coronado's experience that there had been a long and friendly relationship between the Pueblos and the Wichitas.

It is worth noting that on this entire trip across the Plains, 830 miles out and 520 miles back, that Coronado's party met only two small hunting bands, both of Querecho Apaches, and both were along the Texas-New Mexico border. The Spanish found no traces of any other people. Also, Coronado asked the Wichitas for details of all their neighbors and found that they had only two tribes for neighbors, the Pawnees over two hundred miles to the northeast and the Caddoans over three hundred miles to the southeast. They had no knowledge of any other Indians to the north and west of their land. From this evidence of the Wichitas, and from Coronado's own observations, it is apparent that the main Apache movement to the south had not yet reached the Arkansas River by 1541, and that the surrounding Plains contained no hunting bands of the former inhabitants.

The Apache Migrations

Early in the fourteenth century, about the time the Wichitas were migrating up the Arkansas River from the southeast, many small bands of Apaches from the Mackenzie River area in northern Canada trickled southward into Alberta along the eastern face of the Rocky Mountains. They were of Athapascan stock and were rather recent arrivals from northeastern Asia.

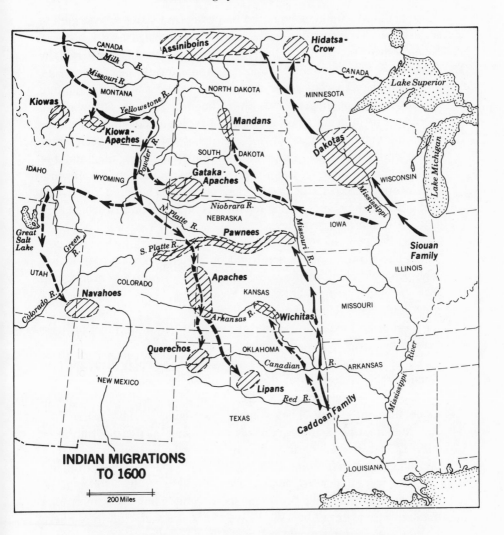

These small hunting bands progressed slowly through the northern forests, nudged onward from time to time by the recurring shortage of rabbits, their staple food. They found that both the hunting and the living conditions improved rapidly as they moved southward, with plenty of game, pleasant open valleys along the streams, little patches of timber scattered through the grasslands that offered shelter and firewood, and an absence of human beings to block their way. The whole of southern Alberta lay empty of men except for a few Kutenais who may have begun to cross the mountains via Crow's Nest Pass to hunt buffalo each summer on the upper drainage of the eastern rivers. Their small numbers in the foothills—well to the west of the Apaches—probably went unnoticed by those travelers.

When the Apaches came out of the woods and began hunting buffalo in the open grasslands they found it to their advantage to combine into larger bands of about fifty people, a more efficient size for attacking buffalo in small herds. Presumably under these much better living conditions they prospered and multiplied, but they did not remain long in Alberta. For reasons unknown they pushed on south into Montana across a belt of treeless plains two hundred miles wide and with much poorer hunting for Indians on foot than that which they had left in the Alberta valleys.

This behavior of the Apaches is the more puzzling because it is counter to that of other Indian bands on the edge of the Great Plains. Those people clung to the woodland fringe instead of venturing out into the wide, treeless grasslands. Had the Apaches emulated them, they could have followed along the woodland fringe to the southeast, for there is no indication that the Assiniboins had moved that far west before the Apaches passed through.

To be sure, once the Apaches had crossed the open Plain and had reached the Great Falls of the Missouri River their route on to the south and east was along the edge of the Plains and within sight of mountains all the way. They were in good game country where they had fine hunting and desirable camping sites along the numerous streams that flowed clear and cool from the mountains, yet they pressed on, driven by some unknown impulse. There is little possibility that they were under any pressure from any other Indians for even the Apache bands that followed them south came along the same trail a hundred years later. The Wind River Shoshoni were still in southern Utah and the Crows would not come up the Yellowstone for another three hundred years or more.

If these Apache bands followed the pattern used by similar pedestrian tribes in historic times, as seems probable, they spent most of each year in their separate hunting bands. These groups remained in the same general area and made some contact with one another from time to time. Then each summer all the bands met in an encampment for several days of visiting and religious ceremonies. At tribal councils the leaders discussed the events of the past year and decided on any future joint activities. In some such fashion these few small bands of Apaches moved onward in a loosely organized group of a few hundred people, not on a definite, sustained march, but rather drifting casually along in a general southeasterly direction.

They crossed the Yellowstone River in the vicinity of Billings and continued on eastward between that river and the mountains to the south, still in good hunting grounds cut by mountain streams and dotted with scattered groves of yellow pine. All along the way they were in good buffalo country. After they passed the northern end of the Big Horn Mountains they came to the Powder River country, rated as one of the finest hunting grounds in all the West, but the Apaches still continued onward across the sagebrush-covered hills and rocky ridges where grazing was poor. At length they crossed the Platte River and finally reached a land of small streams and wide ranges along the Colorado-Kansas border.

It is possible that they stayed here for a period of several years. They must have arrived a little after 1300 or they would have been afflicted by the great drought from Powder River on the south, but they surely passed the forks of the Platte River before the Pawnees extended their string of small villages west to the foothills near Denver, thus barring the way for any small group of migrants. It is possible that when the Pawnees did move out to the west their presence caused the small Apache group to pack up and go farther south until they reached the Texas Panhandle where they stayed. In later times they became known as the Querecho Apaches.

These Indians adjusted well to the buffalo lands on the High Plains of the Panhandle, camping among the herds for about nine months of each year, killing their meat as they needed it and drying a large supply for winter use. Such a small band, working slowly and quietly among the scattered buffalo of a large herd probably did not disturb the animals greatly. The Indians ambushed their game near the water holes or along some defile. There is no indication that they resorted to driving large numbers of animals over the cliffs in a mass slaughter, although they surely took advantage of any buffalo stampede in their vicinity and gleaned the killed and crippled animals left in the wake of the thundering herd, accepting them as gifts from the friendly gods.

Instead of seeking shelter in one of the canyons during the cold months, the Querechos moved on west to visit the Pueblo Indians living along the Pecos River. They camped near the villages, making friends with the farming people and offering them spoils of the hunt, dried meat, tanned hides, and robes in exchange for corn, squash, and cotton cloth. This trade was advantageous to both groups and was carried on over a period of about three centuries.

These Querechos, also known at Vaquero Apaches, were the Indians met by Francisco Coronado in' 1541. They were in a band of about fifty, a pleasant folk and not at all disturbed by the sight of the mounted Spanish explorers. Pedro Castenada, scribe of the expedition, wrote of them, "They are a gentle people, not cruel, faithful in their friendships and skilled in the use of signs." [1] This evaluation is in marked contrast with the descriptions of Apaches a century or two later, after they had been engaged in constant warfare over a long period, wars in which they were usually the aggressors.

Following the Querechos from the Canadian forests were the Navahos who came out of the northern woods and moved down through Alberta along the same route the Querechos had followed. The Flatheads of western Montana have a tradition that they held some of the land on the east side of the Rockies just beyond the entrance to Marias Pass and on to the south for about a hundred miles to Sun River. If they were in this area by the time the Navahos arrived, their presence would have been enough to discourage any small band of Navahos from trying to live there, or from using the route up along the Missouri River into southwestern Montana. So the Navahos passed on south to the Yellowstone River and followed down that stream along the route opened up by the Querechos a century or so earlier.

At the Platte River the Navahos halted, then moved off to the northwest toward South Pass, as though they had found some barrier across their route to the south. Evidently the Pawnees had by that time extended their villages all the way across Nebraska, and these small villages could have looked rather formidable to the scattered bands of Navaho hunters. At any rate they went on west to Great Salt Lake and later moved on south past the Ute bands on the upper Colorado. When the Navahos reached ·Four Corners they found their way blocked again, this time by the Pueblo villages on the Rio Grande. The Navahos made no attempt to go on south through the desert to one side of the Pueblos, but scattered out in their very small hunting bands, probably about ten people in each, and roamed the high desert on a hunting-gathering subsistence. They were in the Four Corners area before the first Spanish colonists came to the Rio Grande in 1599.

While some of the bolder Navaho hunters at times dared to cross the mountains to the east to hunt buffalo, they never moved to the Plains nor did they adopt any of the Plains culture.

The Navahos were followed in turn by the main Apache migration that might possibly have numbered two thousand people. They, too, moved steadily onward in a general southeasterly direction, following along the same route as the Querechos and Navahos, the only feasible one across this land from southern Alberta to the Platte River in western Nebraska for a large body of pedestrians. Along the South Platte in Colorado they found the small scattered Pawnee villages across their line of march and overran them, driving the survivors back to the east toward the main Pawnee settlements. This fighting may have taken several years with the Apaches occupying some of the Pawnee villages for a few years before they moved on to the south.

Just before the Apaches crossed the Platte River, one group moved off a short distance to the east and occupied the south slopes of the Black Hills where they lived for two hundred years or more. They were known as the Gataka Apaches.

The main body of Apaches pushed on well to the south of the Platte and occupied a wide belt of land along the Colorado-Kansas border, an area of many small streams and in the midst of good buffalo country. Here the Apaches developed a few small villages with earth-covered lodges for winter shelter. After a time they began to grow corn, beans, and squash in garden patches to supplement their reserve food supply for the winter months. It seems probable that they first learned about gardening from some of the Pawnee women captured in their raids. They also might have established some early trade contacts with the Pueblo Indians on the Pecos and across the mountains at Taos on the Rio Grande. They could have learned more about gardening from both of those villages. Certainly after 1550 the Apaches had some dealings with the Pueblo Indians, but probably not on any large scale for many years.

One interesting thing about these Apaches, aside from their having passed through such a large expanse of good hunting country to settle in similar country, is that while continuing to live on the High Plains in good buffalo country they gradually changed from nomadic to seminomadic hunters, becoming more and more involved in and dependent on their gardens. This is in marked contrast with the other Indian tribes that settled in villages along the woodland fringe on the eastern edge of the buffalo country and gradually increased their dependence on the buffalo for food. It may be that both the Apaches and the other tribes were reaching the optimum balance between buffalo hunting and crop raising, but simply approaching this state from opposite directions.

Not all of the main Apache migration remained in the new area. A large band continued on to the south, across the Arkansas River and into Texas east of the Querechos. They ranged as far south as San Saba in their hunting. They too built lodges for winter shelter and planted some gardens. They were known as the Lipan Apaches.

After the lapse of many years, possibly a century or more, the last of the Apache groups came south from Alberta. This was obviously the smallest group, and was much less determined to move on to the south. When they reached the Yellowstone Valley, somewhere between Livingston and Billings, they decided it was a good place to live. It was well stocked with game and was free from other Indians. That such a small group could find such a desirable area as this unoccupied underlines again the emptiness of the entire buffalo country in the thirteenth and fourteenth centuries. Since these Apaches lagged so far behind the others it is possible that they found the Wind River Shoshoni in the valley farther to the east around Billings. This tribe came up from the southwest about this time and their presence across the migration path could have been enough of a barrier to stop the newcomers.

These Apaches in time made friends with the Kiowas who lived some fifty miles to the west across Bozeman Pass in the Gallatin-Madison valleys. This attachment became so close and enduring that they were known as Kiowa Apaches from that time on.

The last group of Athapascans to come out of the northern woods were not Apaches, but Sarsi. They reached the edge of the Plains much too late to travel on to the south. By the time they reached the open country in central Alberta they found their way blocked by large, powerful bands of Blackfeet who had come out of the woods to the east a short time earlier. Since the Sarsi had no hope of successfully fighting even one of the smaller Blackfoot bands, and the whole tribe outnumbered them about thirty to one, they decided to be friends instead. Since the Sarsi were a feisty people and delighted in raiding enemies and making trouble, this may have taken quite an effort, but these two groups, so dissimilar in ancestry and language, behaved quite nicely toward each other. The Sarsis conducted themselves so much like a Blackfoot band they were often mistaken for Blackfeet and so many of the Sarsi raids in later years were blamed on the Blackfeet.

These two examples, that of the Kiowa Apaches and the Sarsis, indicate the extreme adaptability of human groups under new circumstances.

The Shoshoni Tribes

About five thousand years ago a band of Uto-Azetecan stock migrated into southern Arizona from the east, possibly from eastern Texas. They settled along the Gila River and its branches and lived comfortably there for about twenty-five hundred years. Then they left the Gila country and moved off to the north, climbing up to the plateau rim. There they split, some moving off to the northeast into the Kayenta area where they settled while others continued on north across the Colorado River and occupied the valley of the Virgin River in southern Utah. This group secured a new type of corn that had been developed in the high plateau regions in Mexico and had spread north, reaching the Virgin River people about A.D. 900. This new variety had many features that made it highly desirable in Utah. It was able to grow and ripen at high altitudes, it was prolific, and was easy to mill.

By using this new variety of corn, the Virgin River people were able to raise larger crops in their fields, thus producing enough food to support a larger population, but in a short time the population increase outran even the increased food supply. Then the colony split into three groups. One of these remained in the old settlement while the other two moved northward. One of these roving bands crossed over the divide onto the drainage of the Sevier River and found a long valley with many acreages of arable land all the way down to the Great Salt Lake. Here they settled in many small farming villages and in time developed a culture called the Sevier complex. They looked to farming for most of their food with corn, squash, and beans as their chief crops, but they also continued to do a great deal of hunting and gathering in the areas around the various villages.

A second group moved off to the northeast from the Virgin River and crossed onto the drainage of the Dirty Devil-Fremont system on the east side of the Wasatch Range. There they spread out along the small streams in a complex of villages raising corn, squash, and beans. And like the Sevier people, they too continued to hunt the surrounding areas and to gather wild foods. The culture developed here is called the Fremont complex. These two groups continued to grow for about two hundred fifty years, spreading out to new lands, the Sevier people moving on north of the Great Salt Lake into the Bear River country while some of the Fremont people crossed the Green River and occupied land along the Colorado River in western Colorado.[2]

Early in the thirteenth century a great drought struck the whole Great Basin area. As the climate became more arid, the rains failed, streams shrank and disappeared, springs dried up. The corn plants shriveled in the heat and produced no grain. In the face of imminent starvation the people turned to the only possible source of food, the high desert. They went out in many small bands, about ten persons in each, and scattered over the hills, hunting and eating almost any form of animal life to be found, including the nourishing Mormon crickets, large insects full of oil and vitamins. They also gathered other insects, rodents, reptiles, and even found a few fish. They gathered and ate seeds from various plants, and several kinds of roots and bulbs. From their practice of grubbing for these they became known later as the "root diggers" which later was shortened to "diggers."

When the Fremont people were forced from their homes in the small valleys west of the Green River, they went east and occupied all the country in the upper Colorado Basin. In time some of them crossed the Continental Divide onto the upper drainage of the Rio Grande, occupying the San Luis Valley. While they depended on hunting-gathering for their sustenance, they still cultivated a few small garden patches where they could grow corn, beans, and squash. They usually planted and cared for a few peach trees near their gardens. In historic times these Fremont people became known as the Utes.

The Sevier group was much larger than the Fremont group and needed a much wider area to accommodate all of its hunting-gathering bands. Almost all of them were forced to go on north of the Great Salt Lake to get past the salt flats and the mountains before they could spread out in several directions. A large band of them moved east to the Green River just north of the Utah line where they split. The larger part went southeast across the mountains into the Yampa Valley of northern Colorado, so named for the nutritious plant growing there in profusion. Some of these people lived in the Yampa Valley for about four centuries, while the rest filtered on south along the eastern face of the Rockies into the series of large parks there. In later years all of these bands combined on the Plains to form the Comanche tribe.

The smaller group left at the Green River moved on upstream and occupied the upper valley. They also went across the Wind River Mountains onto the drainage of Wind River where they could find some buffalo to hunt although they were not on the Plains. Later they extended their hunting range to the north as far as the Yellowstone River and across to the south to the vicinity of South Pass. They were called the Wind River Shoshoni and are classed as Plains Indians although they never did move out onto the Plains. From their hunting excursions they became acquainted with and adopted the Plains culture.

The largest of all these migrant groups of the Sevier people moved north into the upper Snake River drainage before they fanned out to the north and west. Many of them went down the Snake River and took over the western portion of the Snake Valley around the mouths of the Boise, Payette, Weiser, and Owyhee rivers, spreading across the Snake into a large part of eastern Oregon. They never became buffalo hunters or even visited the Plains. Their chief subsistence was the salmon that came up the Snake River from the Pacific Ocean as far as Salmon Fishing Falls near Hagerman, Idaho. They too were known as Shoshoni.

Another large band of Shoshoni occupied the upper Snake drainage around Pocatello, Idaho, and Idaho Falls where the hunting was good and some herds of buffalo were found. This group is sometimes called the Northern Shoshoni. One of their small outlying bands lived to the north on the Lemhi Fork of the Salmon River and was called the Lemhi Shoshoni.

Yet another large band moved on north across the Continental Divide into the upper Missouri drainage in southwestern Montana, occupying the Beaverhead and Big Hole valleys. Some of them later went on to the northeast across the Helena Valley and on to the Sun River country just west of Great Falls. Two of the buffalo jumps they used are still visible. They were later used by the Blackfeet. One is a deposit of about twenty-five thousand tons of rather fresh-looking bones mixed with other residue from many successive large kills.

Later some of the Sun River people moved on north into southern

Alberta. Strangely enough they did not move east into the desirable Judith Basin country only a hundred miles to the east of the Sun River Valley. In Alberta they camped chiefly along the Bow River and the Red Deer River and about fifty to seventy miles east of the front range of the Rockies. They were well settled in this region when the Blackfeet first came into Alberta from the dense forest to the east.

It seems probable that the Shoshoni migration did not extend this far north until the last Apache migration had passed on to the south. It is rather puzzling that the Shoshoni went as far north as Alberta to find hunting grounds where they seemingly were contented, while the Apaches, coming from the harsher north, moved right through the same country as though they had found it undesirable.

In all this country along the western fringe of the Plains held by the various branches of the Shoshoni in the sixteenth century there are two intruding tribes difficult to explain. The Bannocks, related to the Shoshoni and friendly toward them, held some of the country of southern Idaho on both sides of the Snake River Canyon between Burley and Boise. It is possible that they are from the Virgin River settlements and came north much later than the Shoshoni, traveling up through Nevada and reaching the Snake River after all the more desirable portions of the valley had been occupied.

Then there are the Kiowas, distantly related to the Shoshoni through the Tanoan family that founded the Pueblos. The Kiowas lived in the upper Missouri Basin for a long period before the Shoshoni came that far north. The Kiowas were mostly in the lower Gallatin and Madison valleys. It is possible that when the Tanoan people split from the Proto-Shoshoni in Arizona, one of their bands continued on to the north through Utah and southern Idaho into Montana, but it is difficult to assign any motive for such a migration.

The Siouan Family

The Siouan family of Indian tribes looms large in the history of the Plains for it furnished the largest number of Plains tribes, twelve in all, and also by far the largest single tribe, the Dakotas. The twelve tribes comprised about half of the total Plains population in 1780. Although one of the Siouan tribes, the Mandans, was among the first to move to the Plains, another group, the Santee branch of the Dakotas, was the last of all to give up their old homes in the woodland fringe, where they held out until 1862. The Siouan tribes as a whole, and especially the Dakotas, furnished the major portion of the elements comprising the general Plains culture of the nineteenth century.

The early movements of the Siouan stock have not been traced, but these people seem to have been an offshoot of a population center along the lower Mississippi River or in eastern Texas. Their earliest traces so far reported were found in the state of Mississippi. From there the Siouan people moved north into Tennessee, then into Kentucky. Finally a rather large group crossed the Ohio River and settled in Ohio and Indiana. Over the years they increased in numbers and developed a fairly high level of culture. As their population grew, various small bands moved away from the Ohio area to settle in less crowded places. Several of these bands crossed the Appalachian Mountains to the east and built villages from Virginia to northern Georgia, but the bulk of the migrants went westward across the Mississippi River, pushed along by constantly increasing population pressure, and later by the hostile Iroquois.

Using tribal traditions, archaeological evidence, and the patterns of distribution of these people in historic times, a tentative sequence of the movements of the several tribes has been charted. This pattern is subject to adjustment and revision as new evidence on the various groups is uncovered. The pattern presented here is definitely not intended as a definitive solution to the problem of Siouan tribal migration.

Judging from their location far to the northwest, and their indicated length of stay there, the Hidatsa-Crow group was probably the first to leave the Ohio country, moving in small village units first to northern Illinois where they lived for a period of years before they were pushed on by the increasing numbers of people behind them. They moved on to the northwest by a series of stages, their route leading them across the Mississippi River, then northward through western Minnesota, following the valley of the Minnesota River. They were always under some pressure from the next migrant group, the Dakotas, who followed along the same route.

When the Dakotas finally stopped in the western Wisconsin-central Minnesota area, the Hidatsa-Crows, no longer under pressure, settled in the Red River Valley in southern Manitoba where they stayed for a long period, possibly three centuries. They had a long tradition of farming behind them and continued to raise some gardens. They also gathered large quantities of wild foods, but their major item of diet was meat from the large herds of buffalo found in the Red River country until after 1800. During this period these people seemingly suffered very little from hostile attacks. Probably they had no near neighbors.

The Dakotas were much more numerous than the Hidatsa-Crows and were not really organized into a tribe. The group was made up of a large number of separate bands that had a common language, a common culture, and often met together in large assemblies for religious purposes. There is no record of fighting between the various bands.

When the Dakotas settled in the Wisconsin-Minnesota area they scattered out into many small villages near the lakes and rice swamps. Their houses were of heavy-timbered frames with pitched roofs and vertical sides all covered with large slabs of bark. In many of the villages all the people could live in one of these houses. Seldom did they have more than three houses in one settlement.

The Dakotas had been farmers for centuries in the Ohio Valley, but in this northern open woodland they found the wild rice in such abundance in the swamps and lakes that they relied on it entirely for their grain crop and did not even plant gardens for beans and squash. They did some trapping for fur-bearing animals, especially beavers and rabbits, and killed deer and moose in the woods, but their major meat supply came from small herds of buffalo that ranged through the forest glades or pastured on the open prairie just to the west of the settlements.

In this new environment the Dakota population increased to the point that some of them had to move on to new country. A large segment, possibly a third of the total, moved off in a number of small bands and drifted off to the northwest about 1600. They kept to the edge of the woodlands rather than striking off across the open plains. They lived for a time near the Lake of the Woods, then went west across the Red River Valley, keeping to the south of the long settled Hidatsa-Crow people.

These migrant Dakotas later were known as Assiniboins. They occupied the valleys of the Assiniboin and Saskatchewan rivers in western Manitoba. It is probable that this migration took place over a period of many years as the Indians moved out in a few small bands at a time. They evidently made no attempt to intrude on the settled Hidatsa-Crow group, although they outnumbered the latter. If the Assiniboins were moving in small, loosely organized units, it would be to their advantage to keep well away from the Hidatsa-Crow area and avoid any conflict. After they reached their new homes and built up their strength a bitter enmity developed between them and the Dakotas, but this may not have begun until after both tribes had horses, and the Assiniboins were drawn into the conflict between the Dakotas and the Plains Crees.

The Assiniboins lived out in the open country for the most part. There was some timber along the Assiniboin River and a fair amount along the Saskatchewan River, and clumps of trees and plenty of berry bushes along the small streams. As a result of glaciation the whole country away from the rivers was dotted with potholes that held fresh water the year around and furnished breeding places for innumerable waterfowl. To the west and south even berries were scarce, but in compensation the buffalo herds were large and all around the campsites.

Following the exodus of the Dakotas, the next large Siouan group to leave the Ohio Valley were the Mandans. They crossed the Mississippi near the Falls of St. Anthony and built a large complex of villages a short distance west of the river. Here they found good stands of large trees suitable for the heavy timbers that were used to support their lodges. After the heavy frames were in place, smaller timbers were used along the sides and on the roof for rafters. These were all covered with a thick layer of grass and reeds, then the whole structure was covered with a thick layer of earth, the final result—a warm lodge much like that erected by the Pawnees. Cornfields and garden plots were scattered around the villages.

With the passage of time the frames of these lodges slowly rotted and weakened until after eight or ten years they collapsed. When this happened the Mandans moved on to the west a few miles to another suitable spot and built a new village. Always the older houses were in the villages to the east and were the first to collapse. The westward movement then was something like leapfrogging, with the people moving out of the eastern houses and building new ones well to the west of the other houses. This worked very well until they came to the edge of the woodlands and found nothing but open prairie stretching away for a hundred miles to the Missouri River.

Here they paused for a time to rest and regroup, and surely to send out scouts to the Missouri to look for a suitable site for their next move. Such a place was found at the mouth of White River where there were groves of trees along the river bottoms and an expanse of bottom land suitable for their cornfields. The scouts brought the further good news that there were no neighbors of any kind for many miles down the river and nobody at all up the river or in the Plains on either side. The new land lay empty and waiting.

On the Missouri River the Mandans found that the spring floods brought them great quantities of driftwood that could be used for the smaller timbers and rafters of their lodges while the bits and pieces made good firewood. The flood brought an added bonus in the form of buffalo carcasses. Each spring hundreds of these came rolling along in the turbid waters, animals drowned in the spring floods or trapped under the ice when they broke through while trying to cross during the winter. When this bounty came swinging down the muddy stream the Mandans were stirred to a peak of activity. They braved the masses of ice cakes to salvage first the buffalo, then the drifting timber.

After a stay of many years at White River the Mandans moved their villages on up the Missouri. By then some other tribes were coming up the river below them and their timber resources were giving out and they had used up the vast piles of driftwood all along that stretch of the river. Since new lodges had to be built to replace those collapsing after years of usage, it was much simpler to move to a new location where the timber had not yet been cut and build the new lodges at the source of supply rather than to try to float the trees and logs down several miles of the treacherous Missouri, and they had to move upstream because the lower river was becoming crowded with new tribes moving in. So on they went, building new lodges higher up the river, until they finally reached the neighborhood of Bismarck, North Dakota.

During this period of early migration it is probable that the Iowas, Otoes, and Poncas also crossed to the west side of the Mississippi, then moved back several miles from its banks. They built their villages in northeastern Iowa just below the Minnesota line and had the Cheyennes and Dakotas for their northern neighbors. The other Siouan tribes that later moved west and became Plains Indians, the Osages, Missouris, Kansas, and Omahas, remained in the Ohio Valley along the lower Wabash River and in the land on to the east until they were finally driven out in the seventeenth century.

The Algonkin Family

The remaining six tribes that eventually became Plains Indians were all of Algonkin stock. They came from the eastern woodlands of New York, New England, and southern Canada east of Manitoba. The initial Algonkin stock probably came up from the lower Mississippi country shortly after the last ice sheet retreated and left the Great Lakes area and the St. Lawrence Valley exposed. As the Algonkin population increased some bands broke away and spread to the north and west between the Great Lakes and Hudson's Bay. As they moved through the wooded lands they separated into several different tribes, six of which in time reached the Plains and became Plains Indians. These were the Cheyennes, Atsina-Arapahoes, Plains Ojibways, Plains Crees, and Blackfeet. Only one of these, the Cheyennes, reached the buffalo country south of the Canadian border, and was the only one known to have practiced farming.

The Cheyennes came around the lower end of Lake Michigan, probably after the Dakotas had moved through that area on their way to their rice swamps, but before the Iowas and Otoes had crossed the Mississippi River. After a series of uncharted moves they reached the lower valley of the Minnesota River where they settled in small farming villages some years before the first French traders reached that area in the seventeenth century. They raised at least half their food in crops of corn, beans, and squash, and hunted the buffalo just to the west for their meat.

The Atsina-Arapaho group came out of the Canadian woods near Lake Winnipeg after both the Hidatsa-Crow and the Assiniboin tribes had settled in the general area. These newcomers proceeded to occupy a portion of the lower valley of the Saskatchewan between the two Siouan groups.

The two tribes that later became the Plains Ojibways and the Plains Crees were for many years widely scattered over a large area of forest land north of Lake Superior. They lived in small hunting bands, about ten people in each, and depended on rabbits for their staple food, especially in winter. Each of these small bands had its own hunting area. As their numbers very slowly increased they were forced to spread out toward the west because all the forests to the east were already occupied.

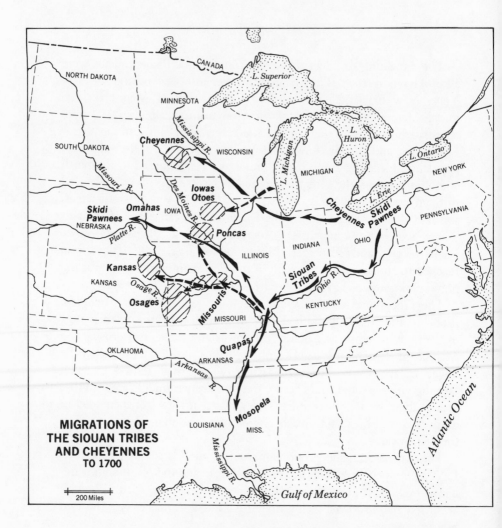

MIGRATIONS OF
THE SIOUAN TRIBES
AND CHEYENNES
TO 1700

On to the north of the Ojibways and Crees and due west of Hudson's Bay were the Blackfeet, also scattered widely in small hunting bands, and with the same pattern of living as that of the Crees and Ojibways. None of these tribes showed any inclination to migrate to the Plains until they were forced from their forest retreats after 1600.

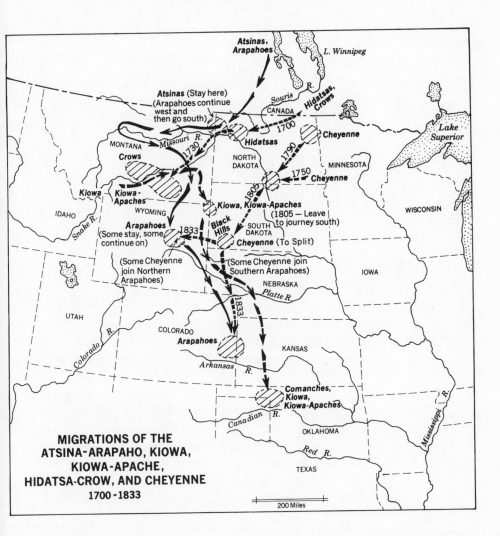

MIGRATIONS OF THE
ATSINA-ARAPAHO, KIOWA,
KIOWA-APACHE,
HIDATSA-CROW, AND CHEYENNE
1700-1833

3

Guns on the Plains

B Y 1 6 5 0 more than four centuries of migrations had given the Plains area only a scant Indian population, with almost all of the newcomers living in farming villages along the Missouri, Platte, and Arkansas rivers. Obviously the wide open spaces of the Plains, still empty of all humans, the teeming buffalo herds, and the spirit of adventure combined were not enough to lure the various neighboring tribes from the woodland fringe. Following the buffalo the year around, trudging day after day across the seas of grass, and defying the strange terrors of the Great Plains had little appeal for these sedentary people, snugly ensconced in their permanent lodges near their cornfields. Only some very powerful new force could expel them from their little villages in the friendly woodlands.

This new force was provided in the seventeenth century by the people in the newly established colonies of the French, Dutch, and English settlers on the Atlantic seaboard. They were in great need of valuable products to export to the mother countries to pay for the many things they needed, but had no money. The fine furs of the Indian country to the west were in great demand in the markets of Europe and brought good prices. They could be had from the Indians for a small fraction of their European market value in trade goods. As a result, fur traders flourished all along the colonial frontier and along the waterways of the interior.

The traders soon discovered that the Indians would pay the most exorbitant prices for guns and ammunition in preference to most of the other goods in the traders' packs. Soon the gun trade was in full swing and all the frontier tribes were armed. A good feature of this trade from the trader's viewpoint was that any Indian buying a gun had to bring in more furs the next year to buy a fresh supply of ammunition, and often the cheap guns needed repairs at frequent intervals, repairs that only a gunsmith could provide.

As soon as an Indian tribe secured a few guns, they used the weapons to attack their enemies to the west, who in turn recoiled against their own western neighbors, so the shock of the guns was transmitted across the mountains, the Ohio Valley, and the Mississippi River, displacing tribes all along the way. When the shock wave reached the populous Ohio Valley it soon pushed some of the sedentary tribes out of the woods and into the strange, fearsome buffalo country. Although only a few explorers and traders had visited the Ohio Valley before 1700, the white man's influence spread far ahead of the advancing settlers and by the opening of the eighteenth century had turned that whole fertile, populous region into a disaster area.

While it was the Dutch traders who moved up the Hudson River from New Amsterdam to supply the Iroquois with guns and ammunition in exchange for furs, the actual use of the weapons rested with that warlike tribe. These fierce Indians had been staving off their enemies on all fronts for some time. Now with their new weapons they embarked on a deliberate program of conquest.

The Iroquois, who were known as the Five Nations to the French, occupied the entire Mohawk Valley in upstate New York. Centuries earlier they had come up from the Southwest, possibly from eastern Texas and across the Mississippi River, then had moved in a northeasterly direction across Tennessee and eastern Kentucky, skirting the eastern edge of the Ohio Valley, already strongly held by the Adena and Hopewell people. The Iroquois finally settled along the St. Lawrence River only to be pushed back to the Mohawk Valley many years later by the powerful, hostile Hurons.

Until about 1570 the Iroquois consisted of five rather weak tribes. Indicative of their hostile nature, they were constantly fighting among themselves and with any other Indians they could find in the adjoining area. Then about 1570 two of their chiefs led them into a strong union, the Five Nations. Once they ceased their continual attacks on each other they found that their combined forces, plus the rigorous training they gave their warriors, soon gave them a big advantage in wars against their neighbors and they started on their bloody trail of conquest, determined to dominate or exterminate every other tribe from the Hudson to the Mississippi and as far south as the Ohio. Later they expanded their scheme to reach from the Ottawa River in Ontario to the Cumberland River in Kentucky. They had the constant assistance from the Dutch traders for their ambitious program. Those keen businessmen were more than willing to trade any amount of guns and ammunition for their price in furs.

The Iroquois began their sustained campaign of conquest and massacre in 1648. By that time they had secured an ample supply of guns and had raised a large, well-trained army. Unlike so many of the western tribes, the Iroquois had regular training and had the troops under some discipline. First they turned their attention to the tribes on their borders and wiped them out one by one. None of these had the foresight or the leadership to unite all of their neighbors in a common cause against the powerful enemy. Instead they sat back, hoping to escape.

As soon as the Iroquois felt their borders were secure from attack, they moved out to the west and continued along the southern shores of the Great Lakes and across northern Illinois until they reached the east bank of the Mississippi. Every tribe that waited for the Iroquois attack was broken and scattered, but some of the tribes had the foresight to move on well ahead of the storm and so managed to survive, losing only their homes and fields. Their flight to safety took them across the Mississippi and many miles farther, into the buffalo country beyond.

One of the first to seek safety in flight was the Skidi Pawnees, close relatives to the Pawnees along the Platte. Their homeland lay just across the mountains to the southwest of the Iroquois on the upper reaches of the Ohio River. When the Pawnee migration from east Texas began, the Skidi, instead of following their brethren north into the Missouri country, went east across the Mississippi and followed the old trail of the Iroquois to the northeast. When the Iroquois had passed to the west of the mountains and had begun to put some pressure on the Skidi, those prudent people packed up hastily and left for the western lands.

They made their first stop about a hundred and fifty miles down the Ohio. There they joined the Omaha tribe of Siouan stock near the mouth of Wabash River. Since these two tribes were from different language groups and different cultures, it is evident that they had built up a friendly understanding over the years, through trade and intertribal visits.

Not long after the arrival of the Skidi Pawnees at the Omaha villages, the advance wave of Iroquois attacks reached nearly to the complex of Siouan villages in southern Indiana and a large migration ensued. First to leave were the Mosopeleos who loaded their possessions into their boats and floated off down the Ohio and Mississippi rivers. They finally came to rest near Biloxi, Mississippi, where they found a spot to settle near a friendly Siouan group. Next the Quapaws took to the rivers and did not halt until they reached a suitable spot on the west bank of the Mississippi in the southeastern corner of Missouri. Neither of these two tribes ever went out onto the Plains to become buffalo hunters.

Soon after the departure of the Quapaws, four more Siouan tribes moved out of the Wabash Valley. They were the Osages, Missouris, Kansas, and Omahas. This last tribe was accompanied by the Skidi Pawnees who had been living near them for a year or two. Details of this migration are lacking but there is some indication that they moved out in several small parties and they made the trip down the Ohio in two or three easy stages. There are several places along the Ohio River where earlier settlers had abandoned their fields near the river. Various bands from the several tribes may have stopped at one or another of these to raise a crop of corn before proceeding on their way to the Mississippi River and on north to the west bank just downstream from St. Louis.

Once they had crossed the Mississippi the tribes found the whole lower Missouri Valley lying open and inviting. Here the tribes went their various ways. First the Osages led the way to the west and found no people along the way from the Mississippi to the open Plains along the Missouri-Kansas border on the upper drainage of the Osage River, for at that time the Apaches were still about a hundred miles farther to the west. The Osages chose a home site several miles back from the open Plains in an area of open woodlands. There they built several large villages and developed their farms. In later years they built several smaller villages right on the edge of the woods close to the buffalo country.

The Osages soon began hunting the buffalo that ranged on the prairies west of the settlements. They must have known about the buffalo pasturing on both sides of the Ohio River, but they had little chance to hunt the animals. The herds stayed in the more open portions of the states of Illinois, Indiana, and Ohio, and in central Kentucky, but some of the Osages may have had some hunting experience as visitors joining hunting parties of other tribes to the north. In Missouri, with the herds near at hand, the Osage hunters rapidly developed their skills and established the hunting pattern so prevalent on the Plains among all the seminomadic tribes. This has been described previously in some detail for the Pawnees and need not be repeated here. It was the pattern of a smaller hunt of about four weeks' duration in June and a larger, more extended hunt in October and November. As their skills developed the Osages were able to secure about half their entire food supply from the buffalo herds.

The Missouris, one of the smaller Siouan tribes, followed the trail of the Osages west until they came to the mouth of the Osage River. They settled there in small farming villages and became seminomadic buffalo hunters, traveling a good many miles each year out to the Plains for meat and hides.

The Kansas went on up the Missouri River to the mouth of the Kansas River, then west up that stream for several miles before settling down and building lodges. They had the Pawnees for neighbors to the north, but the two tribes were separated by about a hundred miles of empty land. About a hundred miles up the river to the west were some of the Apaches in small villages. Seemingly the Kansas had no conflicts with either of these neighbors during the early years of their settlement. They had plenty of good farming land, a small supply of timber along the streams, and herds of buffalo near at hand. They did not have the groves of large woodland trees such as grew on the holdings of the Missouris and Osages.

The Omahas with their Skidi Pawnee friends crossed the Missouri River near its mouth and went on north to the Des Moines River through unoccupied lands until they reached the villages of the Iowas and Poncas. These tribes had first moved into southern Wisconsin, then after a stay of many years, crossed the Mississippi into Iowa and built villages on the west bank quite near the river. After a generation or two they were crowded out of these villages and moved on across to the Des Moines River where they again settled. The three Siouan tribes, the Omahas, Poncas, and Iowas were neighbors along this river for several years, but the Skidi Pawnees moved on at once to the west, crossed the Missouri at Council Bluffs and joined their cousins, those Pawnees who had come up from the south about four centuries earlier to settle in eastern Kansas and Nebraska.

While the Skidi Pawnees were still living on the Des Moines River they must have established friendly relations with their Pawnee cousins in Nebraska, for when they moved over the Missouri to settle among the older Pawnees they were assured of a warm, friendly welcome. Even though these two tribes of Pawnees had separated in east Texas at least four hundred years earlier, and had been separated by too great a distance to have had any contact in the ensuing period, they seemed to have no difficulty in recognizing their common kinship. The two groups blended with no apparent conflict and lived on good terms with each other from then on. The Skidi Pawnees were encouraged to settle as a group on a large area of empty land on the Loup Fork of the Platte, near the Black Hills. There they had as neighbors to the west the Gataka Apaches who had moved into the general area possibly a hundred years earlier and who were addicted to raiding Pawnee villages. It is quite apparent that the Skidis were given the land on the Loup Fork so they might serve as a buffer between the Gataka Apaches and the older Pawnee settlements.

The Skidi Pawnees prospered and multiplied in their new homes. Seemingly this plains environment was more suited to their needs than the hill country on the upper Ohio River. Their numbers continued to increase until they were estimated to be the largest and strongest division of the Pawnees. They soon became skilled buffalo hunters and Plains raiders and held the Gataka Apaches at bay for a hundred years or more.

Although this account of the migrations of the Skidi Pawnees may sound rather farfetched, it is based on the traditions of the three tribes involved, the Omahas, the older Pawnees, and the Skidi Pawnees. The Omaha tradition confirms that the Skidi Pawnees had lived well to the east of them in the Ohio Valley, that they had joined the Omahas on the Wabash, and had accompanied them to central Iowa. The Skidi

Pawnee tradition states that they came from the east with the Omahas. The Pawnees who first came to Nebraska had a tradition that they came from the south before any of the other tribes, and were joined there later by the Skidi Pawnees.

To support these common traditions, authentic artifacts from the Loup Fork village sites include Iroquois-type pottery of the kind found in sites where the Skidi Pawnees presumably lived in the Ohio Valley. It is difficult to account for the appearance of this pottery on Loup Fork unless it was manufactured by a migrant people who had learned how to make such pottery in the upper Ohio Valley, and the Skidi Pawnees are the only migrants that have as yet been identified as having lived in those two places. It is possible that some future archaeological findings will modify the above story, but it does fit the facts known at this time.

4

The Canadian Tribes

WHILE THE DUTCH TRADERS ALONG THE HUDSON were busily expanding their profitable fur trade by peddling guns to the Iroquois, the French traders working out of Montreal were building up their trade with the Indians of Canada, especially those to the north of the Great Lakes in the northern forests, and these woods Indians, like the Iroquois, were interested in securing as many guns as the traders would furnish. As these guns filtered westward through the forests they finally reached the western hunting bands of the Ojibways and Crees just to the east and north of Lake Winnipeg. Armed with these new weapons and combining the hunters from several bands, they formed raiding parties to attack the Hidatsa-Crow villages in the Red River Valley not far beyond the forest edge.

For possibly four or five centuries the Hidatsa-Crow people had lived peaceful lives in this valley. There they could grow some crops and always they could levy toll on the buffalo herds pasturing all around them. These sedentary people soon found that they were helpless against the raiders from the woods who could sneak out, make a surprise attack on a village, and scatter to their woodland retreats before the villagers could gather with their weapons to resist. It was useless to try to follow the raiders to punish them, for they knew all the forest trails and could elude any pursuit. This vulnerability of the small farming village to hit-and-run raiders with no fixed abode has been a problem the world over through all history.

Faced with the choice between slow destruction at the hands of their enemies over the next several years or a flight to new lands still empty of people, the villagers chose the latter. They packed up what possessions they could carry on their backs and fled across the Plains to the southwest, leaving their villages and their valley to the invaders. Away from the river they climbed up to the Plains and trudged off for well over a hundred miles, up the long gentle slope that led to the height of land around Devil's Lake, a land they found much less to their liking than the fertile fields along the Red River. The Dakota hills were high, bare, and cheerless. They offered little protection against winter storms, they lacked the groves and thickets that might supply timber for the lodges and wood for the cooking fires. At this higher altitude the garden crops might suffer from frost any month of the year. Even the buffalo herds usually sought more luxuriant pasturage elsewhere.

After a short stay around Devil's Lake the fugitives were convinced they should move on to better conditions. To the southwest on the banks of the Missouri the scouts found the Mandan villages, peaceful and prosperous, with good gardens and cornfields. On up the Missouri above the Mandans the whole country lay empty, theirs for the choosing. Therefore they occupied the river bank several miles above the Mandans and settled down in well-built lodges, for they had good timber in the river bottoms plus the supplies of driftwood that came down on the spring floods. Their village sites were well chosen, on the high bluffs above the river, while their fields were on the lower lands. From the friendly Mandans they secured seeds of various kinds, including a variety of corn adapted to that area, and they copied some of the farming methods of their neighbors. These migrants had a long tradition of farming and adjusted to the new land with little difficulty. They had been skilled buffalo hunters for centuries and had no trouble securing their meat and robes from the adjacent herds.

Safe from enemy raiders, except for the Mandans, they had no humans in any direction for hundreds of miles, and well supplied with good food, the Hidatsa-Crow people underwent a rapid increase in population. Soon their area became crowded. They could not expand any farther upstream, for the land along the river lay rough and broken to the Montana border, the famous Badlands of the Missouri. When the time came for a part of the tribe to move out to new lands, about half of them went on up the Missouri, then up the Yellowstone, for their scouts had found a fair land, empty of people for three hundred miles above the mouth of the Yellowstone. The group that remained in the old villages were the Hidatsas, while those that moved on up to the Yellowstone were the Crows.

Upstream beyond the Badlands, a few miles beyond the mouth of the Yellowstone the Crows found suitable village sites. They built some villages and settled there for a time. Other bands of Crows moved on upstream twenty or thirty miles before they settled. Each time the lodges started to fall down the villagers moved on beyond the farthest village to build their next homes. In this fashion over a period of perhaps forty years they came to the pleasant, game-filled country where the Powder, Tongue, Rosebud, and Big Horn rivers flow down to join the Yellowstone. There they took up permanent residence, but they no longer tried to raise any crops. Perhaps the hunting was too good. At any rate they did no gardening beyond tending a few small patches of tobacco that they needed for ceremonial purposes. Their hunting grounds on the upper Powder River were considered some of the finest in all the Plains.

After the Hidatsa-Crow people had been driven from the Red River Valley, the victorious Ojibways turned against the Atsina-Arapaho tribe of Algonkin stock that lived off to the west in the lower Saskatchewan Valley. They soon collapsed under the steady pressure of the numerous well-armed Ojibways, and retreated hastily, going off to the southwest to Devil's Lake along the trail of the Hidatsa-Crows. After they reached Devil's Lake, they split into two groups. The smaller group, known as the Atsinas but often called the Gros Ventres in the older accounts, remained on the high lands between Devil's Lake and the Montana border. The larger group, the Arapahoes, pushed on to the west.

The Arapahoes have a tradition that they first went as far west as the forks of the Marias River, about three hundred miles beyond the Montana border and about a hundred miles east of the Rocky Mountains. There they were attacked and driven back by enemies they identified as the Blackfeet. They must have made a mistake here. Although the Blackfeet held all that part of Montana from about 1785 on until they were put on their reservation, they were far to the north in Alberta, north and east of Red Deer River at the time of the Arapaho migration, and the Marias Valley was held by a strong

Shoshoni band. Nearer to the mountains, at the eastern end of Marias Pass, the Flatheads lived at that time, so the attack on the Arapahoes must have come from one or the other of these tribes.

After this setback the Arapahoes drifted off across Montana to the southeast until they reached the Yellowstone River. They made no effort to settle there but went on south up the Powder River and finally found a home in a fairly good area along the South Dakota-Wyoming border just west of the Black Hills. Since neither the Arapahoes nor the Crows report any conflict between the two tribes when the Arapahoes passed through, it is possible that the Arapahoes crossed the Yellowstone near Miles City while the Crows were still many miles downstream in their small villages between Glendive and Sidney.

About the time the Ojibways reached the Red River Valley south of Lake Winnipeg, the Crees emerged from the forest to the west of that lake. Presumably they were a weaker tribe than the Ojibways, and when they reached the open country they encountered the Assiniboins, a much stronger tribe than the Atsina-Arapaho people. Since they could not successfully attack the Assiniboins in their camps out on the open Plains, the Crees joined forces with them and the two became staunch allies in a compact that lasted for a century or more. The Assiniboins seemingly were quite willing to welcome the Crees, for they expected that tribe to supply them with goods from the French traders.

The English traders along the Atlantic coast were frustrated in their attempts to expand their fur trade to the west across the mountains. To the south they were hemmed in by the Spanish, and to the north by the Dutch and French. In order to get their share of the rich Canadian fur trade, they opened up a water route far to the north. They sailed their trading ships to the northwest, passing between Greenland and Labrador, then on south into Hudson's Bay, trading with all the Indians they could induce to come down to the shore. They found furs more plentiful along the west side of Hudson's Bay, for the coast Indians there acted as middlemen, trading their newly acquired British goods off to their less fortunate brethren farther inland and charging them plenty for the favor, but they kept all the guns for themselves.

As the demands of the coast Indians for trade goods increased, they tried to secure more furs by expanding their trapping on to the west through the forests, using their new guns to drive out those trapping bands that had lived there for possibly two or three centuries. Most of these scattered small bands were Blackfeet who had no pattern of organized efforts and their weapons were ineffective against the guns of the attackers, so they gave way, retreating to the west until they were beyond the thick forest and had come into the more open timber near the foothills of the Rockies, where the scattered timber was interspersed with forest glades. There the Blackfeet found new kinds of game, the most important being the buffalo that ranged through the open woods in small bands.

Here was meat more abundant than they had ever known, all they could eat and some to spare once they learned the necessary skills to bring down these great animals. No longer would they have to endure the long winters on an often scanty diet of rabbits. They learned the new hunting methods quickly, probably having the Assiniboins just to the southeast as teachers, who had been hunting buffalo for centuries.

These two tribes, the Assiniboins and the Blackfeet, were on a peaceful footing from the start. They did a great deal of visiting and some trading back and forth between the various camps. A few young men of one tribe might spend an entire season or a year or more visiting their neighbors to go with them on hunting parties and raids. Such a relationship was well established by the 1720s, as is shown by the old records. This visiting often led to more lasting ties when one of the young men decided to marry and settle down with his wife's people.

Although the Blackfeet did not reach the Plains until late in the eighteenth century, they were in the open lands in northern Alberta by 1700, occupying that portion to the north and east of Red Deer River. Seemingly they made a rapid transition from their small hunting-trapping bands to the larger groups needed to cope with the hunting problems among the buffalo herds. When they had made this adaptation, they had little difficulty in securing enough meat and hides for their needs. They lived much better and much more securely than they had in the forests. No longer did the Indians armed with trade muskets ambush them on their trap lines nor did the recurring shortage of rabbits bring them to the verge of starvation in the winter. In this new land under better conditions more of their babies survived and the tribal population increased until they became a large tribe, second in number only to the Dakotas.

As the tribe grew, it had need for wider hunting grounds. These could be had to the southwest, but only if they could drive out the

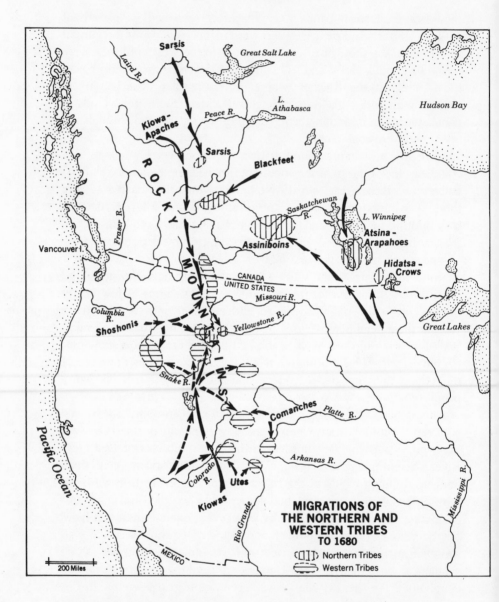

**MIGRATIONS OF
THE NORTHERN AND
WESTERN TRIBES
TO 1680**

Northern Tribes
Western Tribes

200 Miles

Shoshonis that lived there, holding a wide belt of fine hunting grounds
from the south bank of Red Deer River as far south as Sun River in
Montana. The Blackfeet also had disputes over land with the Kutenais
who came across Crow's Nest Pass to hunt buffalo near the mountains,

and with the Flatheads, the Montana Salish, who held a small portion of the Plains just east of Marias Pass.

With their rapid growth, the Blackfeet soon had more warriors than any of their neighbors. Then they became quarrelsome and difficult. They soon had a reputation among their neighbors of being fierce and troublesome, always looking for fights.

In summation, then, not only the Great Plains but even all of the surrounding fringes were entirely empty of men in the year 1200. The complete depopulation of the great expanse was the result of the migration of many bands of hunters from the arid, open country to the moister woodlands to the east. This movement away from the Plains was completed at some undetermined date previous to 1200. Then the flow of population was reversed. Starting with the Pawnees in the thirteenth century, all twenty-seven of the tribes later to be classed as Plains Indians, plus five divisions of Apaches and two of Shoshonis, had moved into position, some of them in the valleys of the major rivers, but the majority just within the open woodland fringe to the east, and close enough to hunt buffalo on the Plains. Only two of the later Plains tribes, the Comanches and the Utes, living in the Colorado Rockies near the edge of the buffalo country, waited until after they secured horses before they too became buffalo hunters.

Among such a large number of tribes with such a diversity of backgrounds and scattered over such a vast area there was understandably some variation in the hunting patterns. The simplest of these, and surely the earliest, was that of an organized group of hunters from a farming village going out to the nearest grazing lands to kill a few buffalo. Such hunts were carried on throughout the year and seldom required the hunters to travel very far from the village or to stay away more than a few days at a time. Seemingly some of the tribes with good crops and with buffalo feeding nearby never felt any need to develop their hunting pattern beyond this point before they secured horses. These tribes were the Wichitas, Mandans, Hidatsas, Crows, a portion of the Dakotas, and possibly the Cheyennes.

Other tribes that began with the above pattern were forced to make some adjustments as their need for buffalo products increased and their regular hunting near the villages over the years drove the herds to more distant grazing areas. To handle this situation the villagers lengthened their hunts, going much farther afield, and set a pattern of two large hunts a year as was described in some detail for the Pawnees. These large hunting parties, consisting of practically every villager able to walk a few miles at a time, were a logical development.

On these large hunts the basic plan of the Indians was to kill a large number of buffalo at one time. This they usually accomplished by driving the animals off a cliff or "buffalo jump." Since such kills were made in warm weather, the hunters needed to get the carcasses skinned out and the meat sliced and on the drying racks before it could spoil. This meant that they needed a large labor force at their command, and the only people available were the hunters' families.

It is easy to understand why the hunters were willing to take their families along on the hunts. Anyone able to walk could help with the butchering and later could carry back a load of dried meat or hides. In time these hunts developed into something resembling a big vacation for everyone and allowed the villagers to roam about on the Plains as long as they did not stray too far from the woodlands. During all this extensive hunting, with the villages left almost unguarded, there is no hint that either the hunting camps or the villages were in danger from enemy raiders, a strong indication that such intertribal warfare was absent because the tribes lived so far from one another. After the Indian population increased and had become more mobile through the use of horses, such raids occurred frequently.

The tribes following the pattern of two large hunts each year with almost all the people participating were the Osages, Missouris, Kansas, Omahas, and, of course, the Pawnees. The Iowas, Poncas, and Otoes probably used the same pattern on a smaller scale.

The third pattern of hunting was that practiced by the nomadic bands. While several of the Plains tribes may have been nomadic before they secured horses only one pure example of such a tribe ever came under the observation of a European traveler. The band observed by the Coronado forces was composed of Querecho Apaches who had come from the north woods of Canada as hunting nomads and continued as such as long as they retained their tribal identity. Usually they camped among the herds, camping away from the feeding animals and causing little commotion. Their hunters killed the two or three animals a week needed to feed the band by lying in wait along the trails leading to the water holes. They then tried to mortally wound one of the animals toward the rear of the line without frightening the rest into flight. When the wounded animal finally lay down to die, the hunters moved in and took possession of the carcass. These hunters also gleaned the dead and crippled buffalo left in the wake of a stampede. At times they also used the buffalo jump, but much less than did the tribes in Canada and Montana.

The main Apache migration followed the Querechos from northern Canada and finally settled in western Kansas. They came south as nomadic hunters, then learned how to build lodges and to raise gardens, probably from captured Pawnee women. They changed from nomadic hunters to village dwelling farmers who hunted the buffalo around their villages. There is no indication that they went on extended hunts on the Pawnee pattern. Before they needed to make any further adjustment in their hunting pattern they secured horses. Their progress in Plains living is the reverse of that commonly expected as the ordinary development of Plains tribes.

Judging from the kind of land they occupied, and from their later pattern, it is highly probable that both the Atsinas and the Assiniboins became nomadic as soon as they were driven from the river valleys about fifty years before they secured horses. No other pattern of living was possible for them on the open Plains along the Canadian border where there was almost no wild food plants or berries and the climate and the soil both were poorly suited to the raising of crops.

Another group of tribes also lived as nomads, but they were not on the High Plains although they did live in buffalo country. All of these lived in the foothills or in the valleys near the mountains, and probably planned their travels each summer to take advantage of the various crops of roots, bulbs, berries, and seeds rather than basing their plans on the buffalo herds, for they could usually rely on finding adequate numbers of buffalo near their harvesting grounds. These tribes were the Kiowas, in the Gallatin-Madison valleys of southwestern Montana, the Kiowa Apaches along the Yellowstone Valley, the Wind River Shoshonis in the Wyoming mountains, the Arapahoes along the western slopes of the Black Hills, and the Gataka Apaches on the southern slopes of those same ranges.

When all of these tribes are mentioned as buffalo hunters and their various living areas are listed, it is easy to fall into the false assumption that they occupied a very large part of the Great Plains. A more accurate picture can be secured by plotting all of these tribes on the map and then indicating the areas adjoining each village over which that group of Indians usually hunted. When this is done, the vast areas of the Plains still empty of people show quite plainly.

5

The Coming of the Horse

WHILE THE GUNS from the Dutch, French, and English traders were disrupting the Indian tribes throughout the woodland area and driving many tribes to seek safety by taking up new homes west of the Mississippi, horses from the Spanish colonies were bringing great changes in the pattern of living to the Indians on and around the 750,000 square miles of the Plains. And just as the guns and their influence had spread far ahead of the advancing white settlements, horses and their influence spread even farther beyond the Spanish ranches on the New Mexican frontier. One great difference between these two disrupting influences was that new guns had to be bought each year to replace those worn out or lost, and quantities of new ammunition were needed each season, and these items had to come from the traders, to be paid for in furs. On the other hand the horses, once established on the Plains, could reproduce themselves, or could be replaced by more horses, stolen, not purchased from the Spanish stockmen. While the traders were willing to sell any number of guns to the forest tribes that the latter could pay for, the Spanish tried very hard to prevent the Indians from acquiring any more horses, even by purchase.

The very rapid adoption of the horse with all its accompanying gear by the primitive tribesmen of the plains produced a large body of skilled, well-equipped nomadic horsemen by the time the explorers and traders of the eighteenth century visited the roving bands of buffalo hunters. For centuries the people of western Europe had considered the Cossacks of the Don River country in southeastern Russia the finest horsemen in the world, and once some of these Europeans were able to observe the Plains Indians in action, they soon rated these mounted warriors as second only to the Don Cossacks, if not their equals. When these knowledgeable observers studied the horse trappings, the gear, and the training methods used on the Plains they concluded that such a highly developed, complex horse culture must have required many centuries for its development. Then when fossil remains proved that wild horses had lived in North America for several hundred thousand years, it was believed that the Plains Indians had tamed the wild horses many centuries earlier and had developed their own complex horse culture long before the first Europeans arrived in the Indian country.

It came as something of a shock to the scholarly world when researchers showed that none of the mounted Indians of the West had owned any horses before the middle of the seventeenth century. It was true that their horse culture had required three or four thousand years to develop, but the Indians had had no part whatsoever in its growth. They had simply borrowed the culture in its entirety from the Spanish colonies in New Mexico when they borrowed the horses, then had added just a few gaudy touches of their own to the trappings. They had also invented a number of appropriate myths and legends to accompany their new acquisition. In this manner they were able to stage the spectacular pageantry that so captured the imagination of the wide variety of visitors who visited the Plains in the nineteenth century.

Before the story of the spread of the horses to the Plains tribes had been researched, documented, and dated, some reputable scholars who knew very little about horses seriously advanced the theory that the Indians really had owned horses as early as the middle of the sixteenth century. Their basis for this estimate was the visit to eastern Texas by the followers of Hernando DeSoto, and that of Francisco Coronado to the Texas Panhandle, both expeditions with horses, and both in the same year, 1541.

According to this theory, so attractive to people with a romantic bent, strays escaping from the saddle stock of these two groups might have survived in the favorable environment and so could have produced enough progeny to stock all the western grasslands in a century or two.

Such a crop of horses could have been large enough to have supplied every tribe in Texas as early as 1560 with a few animals each. Hence any Indians so inclined needed only to capture some of these wild animals and tame them for their own use, being motivated to such a novel action by having seen the Spanish explorers riding across the Plains some years earlier. This theory postulated that most of the Plains tribes of the nineteenth century could well have had horses before 1600.

Although this theory was completely exploded in 1938, many people still cling to it. In 1973 a television show was broadcast, built entirely on the theme of an Indian finding a stray Spanish horse lost on the plains, standing forlornly there with drooping head, still carrying its bridle and saddle. It remained there, quietly allowing the Indian to approach and finally climb into the saddle, to sit there a proud horseman ready to ride off at once in the quest for great adventures. But stubborn historic facts puncture such rosy dreams beyond repair and replace the romantic fiction with the accurate story that begins with the founding of the first colony in New Mexico in 1599.

It is true that after DeSoto's death, the remnants of his expedition did start westward across Texas in an attempt to reach Mexico overland. They traveled as far as the Trinity River in that summer of 1541 before giving up and returning to the Mississippi. There is not a single shred of evidence that they left even one living horse anywhere in Texas.

The much larger expedition under Francisco Coronado that entered the Texas Panhandle from New Mexico that same summer had over five hundred horses and lost several of them. Since there were only three mares listed in the account of this horse herd, it is highly improbable that any of the three were among those horses lost, but even if all three had been lost at one time, and in the company of at least one stallion, they would have been out on the Planos Estacados, an environment rather hostile to horses unused to the climate and vegetation.

But let us suppose that all three mares were lost, and all of them did survive long enough to produce a good crop of colts, and these in time increased until there was a large herd of wild horses roaming those arid wastes. They had to remain far from any Indian tribe if they were to increase to several thousand animals in half a century. In the Panhandle of Texas, where water is very scarce most of each year, those thousands of animals would of necessity have had to use every water hole in the entire area. There they would leave plenty of horse sign that would remain recognizable for fifteen or twenty years. Any horseman passing that way could tell at a glance that wild horses ranged there, even if he never caught as much as a glimpse of one.

This same range was hunted over each year by that same tribe of Querecho Apaches who had seen Coronado and his horses, but in the next sixty years they never mentioned having seen another horse or any horse sign and they went each winter to the Pueblo villages along the Pecos to visit. Several Spanish expeditions crossed the same area from time to time and used those same water holes, yet they never saw any horses or any horse sign. How could there possibly be even a hundred, let alone several thousand, wild horses in the area and no one would ever see them or any trace of them? Yet no wild horses or wild horse sign were reported from that area until 1705, about sixty years after some of the Plains Indians had secured tame horses from the Spanish, and 168 years after the passage of the DeSoto and Coronado expeditions.

The armchair scholars who speak so casually of Indians taming wild horses have little conception of the skills involved and the many difficulties facing the would-be tamer. Even people who are familiar with the process of breaking horses raised in pastures do not realize that other horses of the same stock raised on the open range are much more difficult to capture and tame. The horseman who goes out to drive in a range band needs a well-trained stock horse to ride, a good, stout corral to hold the horses once they are rounded up, and quite a supply of ropes, halters, hobbles, and the like. A young horse right off the range, although it has been running with tame, well-broken horses all its life, will sometimes fight the rope in the corral until it ends up with a broken neck.

Wild horses are even more difficult to capture, and after they are securely corraled they are much more difficult to tame and train. Sometimes an organized group of skilled, daredevil riders on very good horses can drive a band of the wild ones into a well-hidden pen, or can run a band to exhaustion in the open country by using many relay riders on fresh horses to maintain the pursuit until the horses drop in their tracks, but neither of these methods were available to any Indian seeking to capture his first horse.

A third method presented a possibility for any Indian who could invent it on his own. This method involved the erection of a stout fence around a water hole or across the mouth of a small box canyon. Then after the wild band had been allowed several months to become accustomed to the structure, a watcher well hidden near the gate could slip out and secure the entrance as soon as the horses were safely inside. Note that this method required that an Indian who had never seen a fence, gate, or corral, should dream them up, and should know how strong and high he must make his pen to restrain a frantic band of wild animals dashing about once they realized they had been trapped.

This man had to have a large reserve supply of food to keep himself alive for the many days he would spend on his project. He would need to be a young man with no family obligations or he could never find the time away from them for such an undertaking. Also he would have to endure the sneers and jeers from his fellow tribesmen.

Without any tools, except for a few stones, he would need to find and bring in enough timber for his structure. He would have no such materials as wire or nails, but he could use rawhide strips for binding materials together. When he had finished the structure he would need to go off on another hunt for a new food reserve while the sun, wind, and rain removed all traces of the man smell from the whole area. By the time he had his horses in the pen, he would have a year or so of work invested in the project. And there he would stand and watch his captives, not knowing what to do next, for he would have no horse gear, nor any idea of how to start taming such an animal.

Another obstacle to all this, and probably the most formidable of all, was the deeply held conviction the Indians had concerning their relative rank in the world compared to the other animals. The Indians did not believe that the other animals were a lower form of life than man, to be dominated by him. Rather, they were his equals. While many of the animals, including man, killed for food, they must not kill for sport. Nor did man have any right to capture, subdue, and dominate animals for his pleasure. These Plains Indians, well grounded in this pattern of belief, could not become horse owners, horse tamers, or horse users. They had to undergo a profound change in their basic belief, then they had to acquire from the Spanish the necessary skills and gear before they could begin learning to use one tame horse for themselves.

But once the first group of Indians had learned the necessary skills and had become accustomed to using horses, it was a simple matter for them to teach other Indians. It is a matter of some amazement that so many different tribes of Indians from so many different cultures were able to learn about horses and to adjust to their use in such a short period of time for each tribe. While it required 130 years for the horse and the horse culture complex to spread from the tribes adjacent to the Spanish colonies to the extreme limits of the Plains, this allowed only ten to fifteen years for each of the tribes along the way to make this transition, and the whole movement was hampered somewhat during the first forty years by an inadequate supply of horses.

It is obvious that for any Plains tribe to acquire horses, to learn to use them effectively and efficiently in their hunting, and to take over the whole complex of Spanish horse culture in about ten years, as many of the Plains tribes did, that tribe had to start with at least one tame, gentle, well-trained horse, plus a competent instructor with a good supply of Spanish gear. None of these would have been available to a tribe at any distance from the Spanish settlements and faced with the task of learning about horses by first capturing an animal from a wild herd. Only a tribe living on the southern plains and acquainted with the colonists in New Mexico had all of these items readily available.

When the first Spanish ranchers set up their stock ranches along the Rio Grande they drafted young men from the Pueblos to do most of the work. After one of these had worked with horses for years and had become dissatisfied with his lot, his only hope of escaping from his taskmaster was to run off to the Plains and join one of the wild tribes that the Spanish could not control. As he was accustomed to using horses and many weary miles of desert intervened between him and his haven, he naturally took along a few gentle horses to aid in his journey. He also took along several items of horse gear plus the knowledge and skills to produce more. Bits and spurs were the only items beyond his ability to duplicate, for they required metal.

Some of the Apaches who lived in small farming villages in the Arkansas Valley in southeastern Colorado and southwestern Kansas went across the mountains each year to trade with the Pueblo Indians for some of their goods. Later, when the Spanish took over Taos, the Apaches also traded for various articles brought in from Mexico. Over the years the Apache traders became acquainted with many of the Indians at Taos. If one of these happened to be a dissatisfied ranch hand who had become restive under his Spanish oppressor, he might consider the Apache village as a possible refuge for a runaway, especially if the Apaches assured him that he would be welcome among them.

After the Apaches had left for their homes and the Spanish had relaxed their guard, such a man could pack up his gear, take his family and perhaps a few like-minded friends and strike off across the mountain passes along the well-marked trail to the Arkansas River. He could feel assured that once he crossed Raton Pass he would be safe from any pursuit, and could settle safely in an Apache village. Archaeological remains indicate that at least some of these Pueblos chose villages well beyond the Kansas border—a hundred miles or more beyond the first villages on the Arkansas. Spanish records mention just such escapes, including a small group in 1639 and a rather large one in 1642.[1] Probably a good many more went unrecorded and more are a matter of record, but these have not yet been studied.

Any fugitive accustomed to working with horses on a stock ranch would have a very strong incentive to take some animals along, some to ride and others to carry the packs. Thus when he joined the Apaches he was fully prepared to give detailed instruction on the care, handling, and use of horses, and on the making of additional horse gear such as ropes, halters, hobbles, saddles, and the like. Where the Spanish had used rawhide from the skins of horses and cattle, the Indians used buffalo hides. Where the Spanish had used wool fibers from their sheep, the Indians used equally good wool fibers from the buffalo.

Any instruction given by the Pueblo was strictly informal. It consisted chiefly of answering questions by a small amount of explanation and a large amount of demonstration. It was casual, hit or miss, but it was still effective, for all of his audience were deeply interested and paid close attention. Traditions from other tribes, notably the Flathead, Nez Percé and Coeur d'Alene, indicate that often the entire village turned out to spend many hours just to watch the new animals and to observe their movements—to learn what the animal ate, how it rested, and how it responded to handling by people. It is not unreasonable to expect that the Apaches reacted in a like manner.

The importance of using a gentle, elderly, well-trained mare, the kind still known on western ranches as a kid's horse, for those first lessons must not be overlooked. The Spanish seldom gelded any of their stallions, and even a gentle and trained stallion was too much of a horse for any beginner to try to handle. The desirability of acquiring a gentle mare as the first horse for a tribe was stressed in the traditions of the Nez Percé, Coeur d'Alene, and Flathead tribes. No such traditions remain for the Apaches in the buffalo country, for those people were either destroyed or driven out long before any of their traditions could be collected.

Once the young men of an Apache village learned how to handle a horse, especially how to deal with one on the open range, they were ready to raid the animals put out to pasture on the open ranges near the Spanish settlements. In this way they could increase their own horse herd, taking by choice the gentler mares, for they were easier to catch and handle, and also could produce colts. Then there were some special conditions under which an Apache could trade at Taos for a horse. Although the Spanish law was very strict against selling horses to Indians, an animal might be offered in ransom for a runaway Pueblo who had been baptized and whose soul would surely be lost if he were allowed to remain with the wild tribe.

Another source of new animals, too often overlooked by the historians, was the annual colt crop in the Indian herd. Under favorable range conditions each mare can be expected to produce and raise a colt every other year. Of course these young colts must be given protection against predators, including the wolfish dogs in the village that could present a serious problem in a time of short rations. It was fortunate that the most vulnerable period in the life of the colts, from birth to the age of three months, came in late May through August, when the Indians were living on the meat from the early summer hunt and the dogs were well fed on the scraps.

Thus by indulging in some horse stealing and by taking adequate care of the colts, a tribe could build up its horse herd to fifty or so animals in just a few years. To a tribe just learning to use horses, such a number seemed adequate to meet their needs. They were willing to trade off a few to friendly neighbors at stiff prices. The necessary instructions on the care and use of the animals were included as a matter of course. In this manner the Kansas in 1724 secured their first horses from the Apaches, with a French trader at hand to record the event.

Although stealing horses from other tribes later became a common practice on the Plains, indeed, really a game with rules and special recognition for the successful thief, only a few tribes secured their first animals by theft. Instead the horses passed from a tribe to a friendly neighbor even before the first tribe had built its herd up to any great size. It is this pattern of distribution, mentioned in several tribal traditions, that helped speed the distribution of horses to the tribes far from the source of supply, the Spanish ranches along the Rio Grande.

Two other conditions aided the very rapid spread of horses to all the Indians on or adjacent to the Great Plains. Although the area was tremendous, the total Indian population was small, so even a thousand animals, carefully distributed, would have sufficed to give each tribe a small band. In addition, the successful revolt of the enslaved Pueblo Indians against their Spanish masters in 1680 gave the victors many thousand horses. Most of these went to the neighboring Plains tribes in the next two years, some in trade, but most of them to bold raiders while the Pueblos were busily quarreling with others over the division of the other spoils of war.

Old records show that in the period of 1658–1770 horses had spread from New Mexico to the northeastern edge of the Plains in Saskatchewan, and that all of the Plains tribes had secured some of the animals. This rapid spread insured that the horse culture complex of the Spanish colonies was adopted throughout the entire area, for each tribe in turn passed the pattern along before there was time for it to make any significant addition or change. Thus the horses carried a large body of common culture to twenty-seven tribes of diverse racial stock, languages, and backgrounds. Hence when any one of the tribes came up with some small innovation concerning horses, or some other phase of culture, the new item was readily accepted by most of the other tribes, for it was considered only an addition to the common practice and did not represent any basic change in the general culture pattern. This homogeneity among the Plains tribes caused the early observers to assign a common heritage to the entire population of the Plains.

Although in the daily round of living pack animals were really as useful to the Plains Indians as were the buffalo runners, those speedy, flashy mounts have received much more attention in history and fiction. They have been stressed so much that one might be led to assume that an Indian hunter had to have a truly superior horse in order to kill a buffalo in an open chase; but such was not the case. While the superior steed might enable a skilled hunter to dispatch five or six carefully chosen victims in a single run lasting a few minutes, an Indian hunting alone on a mediocre horse and carefully approaching a small band of feeding buffalo could be reasonably certain of closing in on one of the slower animals, or one in the rear hampered by the others. All he needed was one good shot with his bow and arrow or a quick thrust with his lance. Sometimes he might even kill his prey with a knife. Captain Benjamin Louis Eulalie de Bonneville tells of such a kill.[2]

> The long privation which the travellers had suffered gave uncommon ardor to their present hunting. One of the Indians attached to the party, finding himself on horseback in the midst of the buffaloes, without either rifle or bow and arrows, dashed after a fine cow that was passing close by him, and plunged his knife into her side with such lucky aim as to bring her to the ground. It was a daring deed; but hunger made him almost desperate.

In this attack the long blade of the hunting knife must have pierced the lung cavity to cause such a quick collapse, but any deep wound in that area would have brought the animal down in a mile or so if the hunter did not chase too closely. While one man hunting alone might not have much choice in his prey, at least the animal would furnish a substantial amount of meat that would be eaten with relish by hungry people.

As soon as a small village owned one fairly good riding horse, its owner could go out hunting by himself and by using caution in his approach, could be reasonably sure of killing at least one buffalo any time he could find a herd grazing within a few miles. Since the other hunters of the village could all be out hunting on the old pattern at the same time, this one additional animal killed by the horseman represented a substantial addition to the supply of fresh meat, for a bull would yield from 800 to 1,000 pounds of edible meat, tough but nourishing, and the total of such kills over a period of several days easily might equal or surpass the total killed by all the other hunters. One good running horse then might double the amount of meat for the entire village.

In a year or two such a village could usually secure a few more good horses and have some sort of mounts for all their hunters. Working as a team, the hunters could bring down several buffalo on each run, and there would be a number of weaker horses to pack the meat and hides back to the village. A rather unusual hunt by such a group is described in another of Captain Bonneville's stories. He was in his winter camp just north of the mouth of the Lemhi Fork of the Salmon River in southern Idaho.[3]

> In this way they starved along until the 8th of October, when they were joined by a party of five families of Nez Perces, who in some

measure reconciled them to the hardships of their situation, by exhibiting a lot still more destitute. A more forlorn set they had never encountered; they had not a morsel of meat or fish; nor anything to subsist on, excepting roots, wild rosebuds, and the barks of certain plants and other vegetable productions; neither had they any weapon for hunting or defense, excepting an old spear . . .

In the course of four or five days they returned, laden with meat. Captain Bonneville was curious to know how they had attained such success with such scanty means. They gave him to understand that they had chased the herds of buffalo at full speed, until they tired them down, when they easily dispatched them with the spear, and made use of the same weapon to flay the carcasses.

Sometimes, when the hunt had been very good, even the buffalo runners were used to carry small loads of meat while the men walked home, and of course all the women returned trudging along under heavy loads. Only when horses were plentiful could they be used as mounts by the women going out on a hunt, and even then the women almost always had to walk home.

Indians living in some of the better buffalo country came to expect their hunters to provide the camps with fresh meat every day and when a storm or some other happening kept the men away from the herds for several days their families called it a "starving time," because they had nothing but a plentiful supply of dried meat to tide them over. Thus it is evident that the end result of the use of horses for buffalo hunting, even on a small scale, was a substantial increase of the food supply of all the people involved. This in turn led to a rather rapid increase in the population.

In addition to having more food, these people also had more hides to be tanned into leather and robes, or to be made into rawhide, a material with many uses in an Indian camp. The people had plenty of soft, warm sleeping robes, and soft tanned skins for clothing and for tipi covers. Also the tipis could be much larger and more comfortable, for the limiting factor for tipi size was the weight of the skin covering. Since this cover had to be a single piece, it could not weigh more than a single pack. In prehorse days the limiting size was about sixty pounds, but for a pack horse it might be as much as 250 pounds. Also, by using pack horses, camps could be moved more readily and over greater distances, thus giving the people greater choice of campsites with better water and fuel.

As the number of pack horses increased, fewer dogs were needed in camp and this cut down on the problem of feeding them. Horses presented no problem when meat was scarce for they always fed on grass, but the dogs had to eat the same kind of food that people ate, and were first to suffer when meat was scarce. Under the changed conditions more of the puppies were killed each year for food, usually when they were in the "woolly" stage of growth, for then they were considered prime for eating. Many of the Indians and the old-time white trappers rated puppy meat as the choicest they had ever eaten.

The horses were not an unmixed blessing. Although they brought more food to the hunting tribes, they also brought more trouble in the form of increased conflict. The people from the farming villages along the eastern woodland fringe ranged more widely into the Plains with their horses, and stayed out longer on their hunts. As they increased in numbers, each tribe sent out more hunting bands each season. Since all the neighboring tribes were following the same pattern of growth and increased hunting activity, their hunting bands soon began meeting each other and usually both were annoyed at finding strangers on hunting grounds they regarded as their own.

Disputed hunting grounds in time led to armed conflict, although the bands also fought at times just for excitement or for an opportunity to take horses from the enemies' herds. This warfare gradually developed into an elaborate program for winning and displaying honors earned in fighting or horse stealing, and spread to all the Plains tribes as an important, colorful part of the new Plains culture. This topic of warfare and the accompanying rituals will be treated in more detail in a later chapter.

6

The Spread of Intertribal Warfare

WHILE THE NAVAHOS were the first tribe to be mentioned in contemporary documents of the Rio Grande colony as using horses, it is probable that the Apaches on the Arkansas River had a few of the animals even before the Navahos secured their first one. Fra Benevedes, a Spanish missionary in New Mexico, in his detailed report on the Indian tribes of the Southwest, was positive that none of the tribes in the whole area had any horses by 1630.

The Spanish colonial records report the defection of a small group of Pueblo Indians to the Apaches in 1639 and that of a larger group in 1642. It is highly probable that both of these groups, and other fugitives not specifically mentioned, took horses to aid them in their dash for freedom and safety across the mountain passes to the Apache villages in southeastern Colorado and southwestern Kansas. If these runaways did take horses along, they furnished some animals before any other tribes were able to secure any.

In 1659 the Spanish officials at Santa Fe reported a raid by mounted Navahos against one of the villages northwest of that town,[1] the first specific mention of any Indians using horses in the Southwest. But the Navahos could not have staged a raid by trained horsemen in such fashion unless they had owned several of the animals for some time and had practiced riding them. A tentative date for the first horse owned by the Navahos then is 1650, about ten years later than the date for the Apaches. It is known that the Apaches secured a large number of horses during the disturbances accompanying the Pueblo Revolt against the Spanish in 1680. From the tribe's actions at that time it is obvious that the Apaches were already quite familiar with horses and knew how to handle them.

The Pueblo Revolt was the first serious attempt at resistance on the part of the Pueblo Indians against the colony in New Mexico although they had engaged in some bitter fighting against the Coronado expedition in 1540. The first Spanish settlers in the Rio Grande Valley had come north from Mexico in 1599, and had taken over all the Indian farmland in the whole area, some for missions, some for ranches. The Spanish kept the Indians on the farms as workers and for eighty years the Pueblos endured this oppressive Spanish rule, toiling away for these alien masters in their own fields, their freedom of movement severely restricted. The breaking point was reached when the mission priests began a determined drive to discredit the Indian shamans and to interfere with the secret rites of the kivas.

The desperate Indians then organized a revolt against the Spanish and the leaders from all the villages gathered at a central location to perfect their plans. They decided that the fighting should begin in every community at daybreak on the same day with surprise attacks on every mission and ranch, with each Indian community prepared to destroy every settler on the village lands. By attacking at all points at the same time, they would effectively prevent the Spanish from assisting each other.

Then it was decided that thirty days should be allowed for each of the leaders to reach his home and to alert his followers. Each leader then took a leather thong and tied thirty knots in it. Each morning when he arose to say his sunrise prayer, he was to untie one knot. When he untied the last knot, he was to give the signal to his waiting followers to attack. The plan worked without a hitch. The Indians killed all of the hated whites they could find. Then they seized all the property and livestock, planning to divide the loot later among all the villages.

The Spanish were taken completely by surprise. They had had no warning of the gathering storm. No devoted household servant was ready to betray her people. About four hundred of the people died in the first onslaught as they tumbled from their beds and tried to arm themselves. About eight hundred more managed to fight their way through to a common meeting place, the men with their arms and a large number of horses. They hastily packed a few supplies and the whole motley crowd—men, women, and children—set off on the long, weary, desolate trail across the desert to the south and finally came safely to the Rio Grande at El Paso del Norte, the great gap where the river breaks from the mountains.

At El Paso they were safe from pursuit, for the Pueblo warriors had no interest in them once they had left the Indian country. The Spanish camped along the river to await the arrival of soldiers from Mexico. Then they expected to return to their homes while the soldiers subdued the rebels. But the relief force was delayed so the people built houses and laid out fields and so established a new colony at El Paso. In this they acted wisely, for they had a twelve-year wait before the authorities in Mexico City raised and sent a force north sufficient to conquer the rebellious Pueblos.

At Taos the rebellion was especially successful. There the local Indians had plenty of encouragement and some help from a band of Apaches who happened to be present for their annual trading visit. Not only did the Apaches encourage their red brothers in revolt but they also gave practical assistance in rounding up and tending all the bands of range horses they could find, while the Pueblos focused their attention on the sheep and cattle.

When the fighting had ended and all the missions and farms had been occupied by the victors, they gathered to make a division of the spoils that included thousands of horses, cattle, and sheep, in addition to guns, tools, horse gear, household goods, clothing, blankets, and the like, wealth that had been far beyond the grasp of any Pueblo peon but was well within the reach of a victorious warrior. Some dissension in the division was inevitable, for there was little relationship between the number of fighting men from a village and the amount of loot seized near the village, nor did the men who had fought the hardest and longest have time to gather any of the plunder. Also, when the Spanish had organized their retreat and began their withdrawal to the south, they were followed far down the valley by some of the Indians to make sure the fugitives continued on their way. When these warriors finally gave up the chase and returned to their homes, a great deal of the plunder had been distributed.

The biggest problem facing the Pueblos was the equitable distribution of the many flocks of sheep pasturing on the desert lands away from the river. To these Indians, sheep were much more desirable than cattle or horses. Sheep produced both an annual crop of wool and lambs. Slaughtered sheep were good food, and their pelts were valuable. For centuries the Pueblos had spun cotton fibers into yarn and had woven cloth from the threads. They had readily accepted wool as a convenient and valuable fiber, for woolen cloth had many advantages over cotton for some articles of clothing and for blankets. As soon as the sheep were available, each village tried to secure a large flock for its own.

Cattle were of much less value to the village dwellers with their unfenced fields of crops along the river. Cattle were harder to herd than sheep, and needed better pasture and more water than did the sheep. They produced less meat for the same amount of care, and the Indians would not try to milk them. Also the cowhides and the resulting leather were of less value than the sheepskins. As a result, many of the cattle were butchered and eaten in the first few months.

Horses had even less appeal for the sedentary Indians than either sheep or cattle. While horses appealed greatly to the tribes living in the buffalo country, around the farming villages they were a continual nuisance. They were even harder to tend than the cattle, and required more grass and water. So the Indians concentrated first on taking care of the sheep and paid little attention to the horses. When they finally had some time to consider the horse question, they found that there was no longer any question. Their neighboring tribesmen from the buffalo country, Apaches from the Arkansas Valley and from the Texas Panhandle and the Utes and Navahos from the north, had given the answer by removing most of the horse herds from the valley and taking them so far away they no longer ate the sheep pasture or invaded the corn fields and gardens.

In 1680 the Utes and Navahos were still friends. They had come down from the north, presumably on a trading visit, then stayed around for the excitement. While the Pueblos were busy with their quarrels with each other these northern neighbors swept the ranges north and west of Taos clean, and went back home with a thousand or more new horses. Meanwhile the Apaches were driving thousands more in several bands across the mountain passes east of Taos, or southeast from Santa Fe, until they could go around the base of the mountains and on to their own country.

The Apaches returned from time to time to round up any stray bands they had missed on the higher ranges. They probably had some company from the Lipan and Querecho Apaches from Texas in clearing the ranges south to Albuquerque. In the course of two years all these Apache bands together might have secured ten thousand or more horses.

This sudden increase in their herds brought an embarrassment of riches to the Apaches who had been limited to a few hundred animals up to this time. Now they were wealthy, with herds too large to be handled by their old pattern, with large bands of horses scattered widely over the open ranges and needing some attention every few days. Their problems were more serious because they had no natural barriers on any side to help restrain their stock.

Not all of the Apache villages had sent people to Taos to trade, so the returning warriors with all those extra horses had an opportunity to trade off many of the animals to their friends and neighbors in other villages. Horses were so plentiful for a time among the Apaches some of them were passed along to other tribes and soon found their way eastward to the Wichitas and Osages.

For about two years the Apaches could replenish their herds with the strays from the Rio Grande, but then those ranges were empty. The Apaches soon began to feel horse poor, for they had enjoyed the prosperity brought to them by their horse trading. Although they now owned many more horses than they had a few years earlier, their herds were much smaller than they had been just the year before. There were no more horses to be had in New Mexico until after the Spanish colonists returned with the soldiers in 1692, so the Apaches turned their attention to the older settlements of Spanish farmers deep in Mexico. They crossed the Rio Grande well below El Paso and rode far up the Conchos River to the plateau country beyond where they stole several hundred animals in 1686, probably their first big raid into Mexico and the first on record of any Plains tribe so far to the south. Once the Apaches had set the pattern such raids continued steadily for about two centuries with the Comanches taking over after they had driven the Apaches from the Plains.

The Apaches, in bringing horses to the southern Plains, also brought trouble and warfare. As early as 1650 the Spanish officials at Taos started reporting the trading of Pawnee captives by the Apaches, who also brought in a runaway Pueblo once in a while, or someone they claimed as such, and so could be considered as eligible for ransom by the Spanish officials on the grounds that the person had probably been baptized before he ran away.

The Spanish needed very little proof in such a case and under this plan ransomed a few Indians each year although most of them brought to Taos and sold there really were captives from Plains tribes that had never seen a missionary. From 1680 until 1692 this slave trade was interrupted, but it was resumed as soon as the Spanish returned from the south. Even then the yearly purchases of slaves totaled only a few people. Hence it has been easy to exaggerate the total number of slaves brought in by the Apaches over their entire trading period, 1650–1720, by ignoring the years of little trade and that twelve-year period of no trade.

During this period the Apaches did raid many Pawnee villages, killing off the men, carrying away the women and children, destroying the lodges, and carrying off anything of value. A few such raids against any one village destroyed it entirely, and any survivors had to move away to join some other band. Several of the sites of these early Pawnee villages have been excavated and studied, with the evidence pointing up the fact that most of those in the west had been small, with perhaps fifty people in each. A completely successful Apache attack against such a small group would kill off most of them, leaving twenty or fewer captives to be carried away. If a writer stresses the large total of Apache raids over a century or so he might easily overestimate the total Pawnee losses. Although the Pawnees did lose all their western villages and quite a few people during this period, the tribe as a whole appeared to increase in population.

One Pawnee site in particular, in Ash Hollow in western Nebraska, was taken over by the Apaches in 1684,[2] after many years of conflict between the two tribes. Hence it would appear that the Apaches did not make many attacks on villages east of Ash Hollow until after that date, and this in turn indicates that the Apache attacks on the Pawnees were stepped up in frequency after the Apaches secured their large supply of horses during the Pueblo Revolt. In this fighting the Apaches appeared to be the aggressors although they had no real need for the Pawnee captives or for enlarged buffalo hunting grounds.

All of these Apache raids were on a small scale, with a little band of warriors out for excitement and loot. They were not the work of large, well-organized war parties. Raids were usually conducted by the younger men led by one of their number who felt lucky, or who had received some sign or omen, usually in a dream. He then told the others in the camp or village of his dream and announced his plans for a raid and invited anyone who was interested in following him to join the party. If he happened to be a young warrior with little experience he might have to be satisfied with only ten or fifteen followers, but if he was an older man with a good reputation for leading successful raids he might even attract men from other villages in the area and secure a hundred men.

The objectives of a raid were to secure some loot, take a scalp or two, and bring back a few captives, and above all, to accomplish this without getting any of the war party killed. Hence the attackers relied heavily on a surprise, making a dash into the village for possibly five to ten minutes of action, then beating a hasty retreat before the villagers could retaliate. Seldom did any of these raids end in a real fight, and during this period never were they aimed at the destruction of a village and so taking over the surrounding hunting area. When a village finally succumbed to the enemy and the survivors abandoned the site, it was usually the result of a series of attacks over a period of years.

A war party of ten to a hundred men, all well mounted and well armed, who were going against a village of fifty people, only ten of whom were fighting men, and those were scattered among their lodges and unprepared for immediate resistance, had a great advantage. Just as in the case of the Iroquois raiders against the Siouan villages in the Ohio Valley, these Apache raids give added emphasis to the extreme vulnerability of small farming villages to surprise attacks by highly mobile raiders, a vulnerability that has been a constant factor in the lives of men ever since some of them began settling in the villages. Always the sedentary farming folk have been helpless against roving fighters. If the farmers tried to organize a force to strike at the enemy in his own land, they found the foe too elusive. If farmer-warriors were used to patrol the area around their villages to intercept the attacks, the farming suffered and the people went hungry. If the farmers did not go to the fields in armed groups, with some of them always on watch, they were open to a surprise attack.

In the case of the Pawnees, they were in constant danger when they went out in large groups on foot to hunt the buffalo. The most critical time came just after they had made a kill and all the people were busy with the butchering. During the period 1680–1720, when the Apaches had a large number of horses and the Pawnees had very few, it was difficult for any Pawnee war party to make a surprise attack on an Apache village and return safely across the open plains on foot. Their only recourse against the constant Apache attacks was to abandon their small outlying villages along the western part of their holdings and retreat toward the east.

For at least twenty-five years the Apaches were the dominant group in all the buffalo country from the Pawnee villages to the Rocky Mountains. Then about 1700 came a sudden, dramatic change. The Comanches and Utes emerged from their valleys in the Colorado mountains as mounted warriors and attacked the Apache villages along the Arkansas River.

When the Navahos moved south from Great Salt Lake to the Four Corners area it is assumed that they passed to the west of the Utes in western Colorado, for there is no tradition in either tribe of any enmity between the two at this stage. Then as the Navahos began trading with the Spanish settlements, securing manufactured goods from Europe in addition to the Pueblo products, the Utes joined them on trading excursions. The Spanish officials reported the presence of such mixed trading parties at Taos, and stated that there was some intermarrying between the two tribes, indicating a rather long period of friendship. Obviously the Utes secured their first horses from the Navahos, probably as early as 1660.

Also it was about 1660 when the southern bands of Utes moved across the mountains to the upper Rio Grande and occupied the San Luis Valley by the 1670s. From this vantage point they could visit Taos for their purchases without going through Navaho country. The Spanish records indicate that during the Pueblo Revolt there were parties of Utes around Taos who helped themselves to many bands of range horses that were loosely guarded during those troublesome times. This sudden large increase in the Ute horse herds made them more powerful until they decided they no longer needed to defer to the Navahos. About 1690 friction between the two tribes had built up until it developed into outright war with each tribe mounting raids against the other. The Navahos complained to the Spanish about this unfriendly behavior on the part of their former allies, but to no avail. All of this development was among the southern Utes. The northern

Ute bands, comprising the major portion of the tribe, remained along the upper Colorado River across the mountains from the area of conflict.

During the latter part of the seventeenth century the southernmost Comanches near Salida were the poor country cousins of the southern Utes in the San Luis Valley just across a mountain range. The Comanches were of heavier build than their relatives and had short, stubby legs, making them poor at walking and no match at all for longer-legged Indians in the open country such as the buffalo plains.

After the Utes had built up their horse herds with the animals captured from the disorders around Taos, they had so many that they could spare a large number at a good price for their Comanche neighbors. With this help from their good neighbors, the Comanches became well-mounted, skilled horsemen by 1700. With constant practice the Comanches continued to improve until in the nineteenth century they were considered the best of the Plains horsemen and equal to the Don Cossacks of southern Russia who until then were considered the finest horsemen the world had ever known.

Mounted bands of Utes from the San Luis Valley united with the Comanche horsemen to go on regular buffalo hunts out onto the Plains to the east of their mountain valleys. Their trail led down the Arkansas Valley where they found several small Apache villages in the foothills around Pueblo and off to the south near Trinidad. These they raided for food, horses, and slaves. In vain the Apaches called on the Spanish governor at Santa Fe for some protection and help. The Spanish would do nothing unless the Apaches first became Christians and promised to settle near the missions that would then be established in their land. Once the Apaches had been converted, the governor would send word to the viceroy in Mexico City asking for permission and funds to establish the missions and to build a presidio for the soldiers who would then be sent to protect the new converts. Thus even when the Spanish were willing to help, this long, slow process of official procedure, hampered by bureaucratic red tape, required years, while the Apaches needed help immediately if they were to survive. Seemingly they could not help themselves by giving up their attacks on the Pawnees and assembling their whole strength against these new enemies, a condition stemming from their very loosely organized bands. In this time of crisis no great leader arose to bring the scattered bands of Apaches together for the common good.

The Spanish shelved the whole problem until the Utes and Comanches increased their raids when they were finally threatening Taos in 1716. Then the aroused officials sent Spanish troops to follow the raiders, such an unexpected move that the troops were able to surprise the Indian camp and take some captives who were then sold south into Mexico. In retaliation the Utes and Comanches staged several heavy raids in the next two years, killing several Apaches and driving the rest toward Taos where they built new villages.

To counter these new raids, the new Spanish governor, Valverde, marched out from Santa Fe in 1719.[3] He found several abandoned Apache villages, but when he reached a camp that the raiders had left only a short time before he was careful to follow their trail so slowly that he was in no danger of overtaking them. Valverde's report indicated that the Apaches had all been driven from southeastern Colorado by 1719 by the Comanches who used the same tactics against the Apaches that those Indians had used so successfully against the Pawnees.

When the Comanches from the Salida area demonstrated that they could live well in the buffalo country as nomadic hunting bands, their success interested several other bands in the mountain valleys to the north. Soon they too had moved to the Plains in the search of better hunting and better living. All of these Comanche bands, in their efforts to take over a wide range in the buffalo country, mounted attacks against the Apaches and any other tribe that ventured too far out onto the Plains. They captured many women and children in these raids and incorporated them into the Comanche bands. There was a high proportion of older girls and women among such captives, for they were the most prized and so less likely to be wounded or killed when a village was attacked. With such a large number of females of child-bearing age and with plenty of buffalo meat to feed them, the villages and bands prospered and increased rapidly in population as more children were born and more of them could be raised to maturity. As the Comanche bands increased in numbers, they spread out to the east and south, expanding their hunting grounds at the expense of the Apaches in Kansas, western Oklahoma, and northern Texas.

Much of the Comanche prosperity after 1725 stemmed directly from the international rivalries in Europe where France and Spain were often on opposite sides of any question of international concern. The jealousy of the two governments toward one another extended to the colonies in North America where each one was deeply interested in expanding its holdings at the expense of the other. Spain during the entire seventeenth century had held New Mexico and had extended its influence to some of the adjacent Plains tribes through trade. They had no competition until the French moved into the lower Mississippi country.

The French established the colony of Louisiana on the Gulf of Mexico and began sending regular trading parties up the Mississippi. This water route, extending through the Great Lakes to Quebec, was a real benefit to the French traders. It enabled them to work along both banks of the Mississippi and up several of its western tributaries, especially the Missouri, Arkansas, and Red rivers.

Although the French traders during this period made most of their profits from furs, they added a goodly sum to their gross profits by buying slaves from the Indian tribes along the rivers for resale to the plantation owners along the Gulf Coast. Indian tribes with captives much preferred attractive trade goods to their victims, for they could always go out on another raid and so replenish their supply of slaves. Although the French traders were not organized or equipped to handle very many slaves on a single voyage, they could always find some room in the boats for a few each time they floated down the river to market. The rather scant records on this trade in Indian slaves usually speak of these unfortunates as Panis, a variant spelling of Pawnees, and indicate that most of them had been purchased from the Osages, Poncas, Iowas, and Otoes.

As the French trade with the Indians along the Mississippi increased and more men were engaged in the trade, some of them sent back written reports on the Missouri River Valley and the tribes living there. (These reports furnish the first authentic material on this region.) After a time the French extended their trading voyages to some of the tributary streams. By 1719 they were paddling and cordelling up the Missouri to deal directly with the Kansa and Pawnee tribes.

This trade extension brought a sudden, drastic change in the slave-buying pattern, for the fur men could not expect to be received as friends in the Pawnee villages while they were purchasing Pawnee captives from the Iowa tribes to ship out to the slave market in New Orleans. This difficulty was soon overcome by switching from buying captive Pawnees to buying captive Apaches. The Osages and Pawnees were able to furnish a supply of these in return for guns and ammunition that would aid them in securing new captives, for the firearms gave the Pawnees the advantage over the Apaches, more than offsetting the Apaches' horses. But this new arrangement was in conflict with the broad policy for North America that had been drawn up by the high officials in Paris, who envisaged a long-range plan for extending French influence to the Plains by making a firm alliance with a powerful Plains tribe, and who decided that the Apaches living in western Kansas should be considered first as that possible ally. They did not know that the Apaches by that time were dwindling rapidly under the Comanche attacks and could be of little use to the French or to anyone else.

Both the fur men along the Mississippi and the French officials at New Orleans were strongly opposed to the new plan. When E. V. de Bourgmont, an experienced frontiersman who knew how to deal with Indians, was delegated by the Paris officials to go up the Missouri, make friends with the Apaches, and make the best alliance with them that he could, he was hampered at every turn by the New Orleans group, for by this time most of their slaves from the Missouri trade were Apaches and any such alliance would put an immediate end to their whole slave-trading pattern. While most of their opposition to having the Apaches as French allies stemmed directly from their own selfish interests, they were correct in evaluating the Apaches as poor candidates for the role that the Paris officials had chosen for them.

After several delays, Bourgmont finally reached the Kansa villages early in the summer of 1724.[4] He found the Kansas ready, even eager, to make a lasting peace with the Apaches. They expected that such a pact would bring prosperous trade relations between the two tribes, and would give the Kansas a golden opportunity to buy some Apache horses that the Kansas needed badly for their buffalo hunting, for up to this time they had not been able to secure any horses from any of their neighbors.

When the time came for the early buffalo hunt, the Kansas combined their hunting trip to the west with the trip Bourgmont wanted them to take to the Apache villages. Bourgmont had several packs of trade goods for presents to the Apaches and he wanted the Kansa women to carry them for him, taking their pay in goods. This the women were pleased to do, so they loaded up with all Bourgmont's packs, all their own camping gear, food supply, and spare clothing.

They had five hundred dogs along under packs to take a share of the load. In addition to the dogs, the hunting party included 14 war chiefs, 300 warriors, 300 women, and 500 children. On this trip Bourgmont indicated that none of the Kansa people were left behind.

With Bourgmont and his welcome supply of trade goods to pave the way, for he had much better goods at better prices than the Apaches found at Taos, good relations were quickly established between the two tribes, strangers to each other up to this time. They all fell to feasting with the Apaches providing the vast amounts of buffalo meat needed for such an occasion. When they finally met in the great council, they were all in an agreeable mood, and soon had made a friendship pact. Then the Apaches traded a few horses to the Kansas, probably paid for in the most part by the goods Bourgmont had given the women for transporting his loads.

The French and Apaches also made a pact of friendship and mutual assistance. Bourgmont then supplied the Apaches with guns and ammunition to be used against the Comanches. After several days of festivities, the entire meeting adjourned to the Kansa villages a hundred miles away on the Missouri when the Apaches accepted the Kansas' invitation to visit the great river and the beautiful valley, the only record of any Apache tribal visit beyond the eastern boundaries of their land.

For all the friendliness and goodwill engendered that summer, the alliances were of little real value to the Kansas, the French, or the Apaches. The Kansas probably profited the most, for they did get several horses for their men to use in hunting. The Apaches, emboldened by all those new guns, set right out to destroy some Comanches. They surprised a Comanche hunting camp and scored a small victory, but in retaliation the Comanches mounted a large number of raids against the Apache villages in the next three years. Under this continued heavy pressure by their enemies, the Apaches soon wilted and began deserting their villages and moving off to the south. By 1727 they had abandoned all their holdings in western Kansas. Their raids against the Pawnees were at an end, but they still were within range of Comanche attacks.

As soon as Bourgmont left the frontier, the French at New Orleans undermined all his work. His trading post, Fort Orleans on the Missouri, was abandoned. French traders on their next trips upriver to the Osages and Pawnees resumed their purchases of Apache captives, and in order to increase the supply of captives, traded guns in ample numbers to the raiding parties so they might be more successful and might make bolder raids in the future. A new trading post was built near the Kansa villages to further encourage the attacks on the Apache villages. The Kansa tribe then rather abruptly ended their new friendship pact, finding the profits from the new arrangement more to their liking. Then too, with their new horses, they wanted more hunting grounds toward the west, lands previously preempted by the Apaches. Within two years after the Kansa post was built, the Apaches had been driven completely out of Kansas and neither the Kansa tribe nor the Osages had any more opposition to their expanding their hunting to the west until the Comanches finally decided to take over some of the land vacated by the Apaches.

On the Arkansas River the southern Pawnees and the Wichitas, then often called the Jumanos, had large farming villages where the Comanches came at times to trade. The French fur men came up the river, bringing in a good supply of guns with their other trade goods. The Wichitas and Pawnees made some profit from this trade. In addition they insured themselves against Comanche attacks. The Comanches, for their part, were pleased to be able to secure a reliable source of guns and ammunition without having to depend wholly on the Spanish at Santa Fe and Taos. The Spanish grudgingly parted with only a few guns at high prices, and neither their powder nor their goods were of the best quality. The French supplied the arms in much larger quantities and of better quality. They also gave more in trade for the horses brought in by the Comanches.

So for the first time the Comanches had what they considered an adequate supply of guns, and a place where they could purchase good ammunition when they needed some. They also had a rapidly increasing population as successive bumper crops of babies grew to adulthood. Made proud by their prosperity and stimulated by a desire for more living room, the Comanches then turned on their friends of long standing, the Utes, and attacked them at every opportunity. In about twenty years the Comanches had driven the Utes back into the mountains until that tribe no longer dared to camp on the Plains for months at a time hunting buffalo. Penned in their mountain valleys, they continued sending hunting parties among the buffalo herds for another hundred years or more, but they made these hunts in quick dashes, securing some meat and hides before retreating hastily into the mountains. Since they dared not tarry on the Plains, they never became nomadic buffalo hunters, but they borrowed enough of the common Plains culture to be classed as Plains Indians.

The Comanches had a rather strong feeling of enmity against the Utes for no apparent reason. They mounted attack after attack against their former friends when they had nothing to gain by such actions until the Utes called them "the people who fight us all the time." After these southern Utes became deeply involved in this constant fighting with the Comanches they lost both power and prestige. Meanwhile the northern Utes, who held most of western Colorado, enjoyed a comparatively peaceful life and in time became the more important segment of the tribe.

Once the Comanches felt they had the Utes penned in the mountain valleys, they turned their attention to the Apaches south of the Arkansas River. Soon they had cleared all of the Canadian River country of these enemies. The survivors fled to the Pecos River in eastern New Mexico only to come under further Comanche attacks. By 1777 all of the surviving Apaches of the original central group had moved on to the west. They crossed the Rio Grande and sought refuge in the White Mountains at the head of the Gila River in eastern Arizona. There they were finally safe from Comanche attacks, but they had to give up buffalo hunting and so never had any more chance to become one of the Plains tribes even though they had held a large part of the buffalo country for about three centuries.

In all this fighting the Comanches seemed to have the destruction of the Apaches as their prime objective. It is not clear whether they planned a long-range campaign, with the enlargement of their hunting grounds as the major objective, or whether they enjoyed fighting and just secured the extended holdings as an unplanned bonus. A purposeful campaign of this sort lasting for several years was unusual for a people living in scattered bands with no recognized common leadership as was the case with the Comanches. Their various bands were bound together with few ties beyond a common language and a common hunting area.

The southernmost tribe of the Apaches, the Lipans, had come south as one prong of the advance guard of the main Apache migration. When the Querechos reached the Texas Panhandle and remained there, the Lipans passed well to the east of them and eventually staked out their claim to hunting grounds as far south as the Colorado River of

Texas. It is probable that the Lipans moved more slowly than the Querechos once they reached Kansas. These two groups of Apaches had to infiltrate into hunting grounds used occasionally by other tribes that had been in Texas for a long time, in all likelihood the descendents of those early people who built the hearths at Lewisville some thirty-seven thousand years earlier. Both of these Apache groups came south in small hunting bands and had to be content with the less desirable portions of the Texas Plains for two centuries or more.

After the Lipans finally reached the upper valleys of the Red and Colorado rivers, they built a number of small villages and settled into a seminomadic life. Then in the latter half of the eighteenth century they secured horses from their kinsmen to the northwest who had taken the animals from the Spanish colonies in New Mexico. It is probable that the Lipans had very few, if any, horses until after 1680 when the Pueblo Revolt allowed the Apaches to secure several thousand animals in a year or two.

The mounted Lipans soon were staging raids against the Caddoan villages to the northeast on the Red River. They took their captives to New Mexico to trade to the Spanish, who at first refused to purchase the few children offered for sale on the grounds that such transactions were against Spanish law. When the Lipans immediately killed the children, the Spanish were shocked, and changed their policy to allow such captives to be purchased. For about thirty years the Lipans, because of their horses, were able to terrorize the Caddoan villages. Then French traders from New Orleans came up the Red River and brought guns to the Caddoans. With these new weapons the Caddoans held the upper hand and were able to drive the Lipans back. They also captured a number of Lipans to trade to the French slavers.

About 1750 the southward-moving Comanches, also armed with French guns, began attacking the Lipan villages. Under the combined assaults of the Caddoans and Comanches the Lipans were soon in desperate straits. They ceased their small raids on the Spanish settlers near San Antonio and soon began asking the Spanish officials there for help.[5] Specifically, they wanted the Spanish to place a strong force of soldiers in a fort on the Colorado or San Saba rivers to hold back the Comanche war parties.

The Spanish authorities at San Antonio lacked both the funds and the soldiers necessary for such a venture. They had to relay the request to the viceroy in Mexico City who then sent it on to the ranking officials in Madrid. Owing to the official red tape and the slowness of communications, the request took three years to be approved and the notice of the approval, together with the necessary funds, to reach Texas. The high officials had made a few changes in the plan. They insisted that a mission be built first, with a few soldiers to protect it. The Lipans then were expected to come in to the mission, become Christians, and settle permanently on small farming plots in the San Saba Valley.

Construction of the mission finally got under way in the spring of 1757 to the delight of the Lipans, who stayed around the place most of the summer to watch the builders in action. Then when the building was almost finished in the early fall and the friars suggested that it was time for the Lipans to move in and build their own lodges, the Indians packed up and went off to hunt buffalo and to spend the winter months in their usual haunts on the headwaters of the Red and Colorado rivers.

When spring arrived in 1758 so did the Comanches. In March a large war party rode up to the mission. Many of them were carrying new guns just bought from the French traders at the Caddoan villages. After they had inspected the new mission they announced that as long as the friars were helping their enemies, the Lipans, they automatically became enemies of the Comanches and would be treated as such.

The Comanches had brought along from the Caddoan villages about a thousand warriors of the Tawehash tribe and had sufficient force to overwhelm the small Spanish post. They killed the friars and their helpers and destroyed the new mission buildings.

In retaliation the Spanish organized a powerful, well-equipped force of six hundred men at San Antonio. They marched north under the command of Captain Diego Ortiz Parilla in search of Caddoan villages to attack, for they knew it was hopeless to try to reach the roving Comanches out on the Plains. The Lipans, impressed by this show of force and hoping for some of the spoils of war, furnished a thousand warriors to help the soldiers.

Lipan scouts led the Spanish forces to a small Caddoan village that succumbed to a surprise attack and about sixty Caddoans were killed. Then the army marched on a large Caddoan town that was fortified with a deep ditch and palisades and garrisoned by about five thousand Tawehash and Comanches. In spite of strong attacks, aided by the small bronze cannons of the Spanish, the army could not breach the walls and had to retreat, with the enemy following closely on their heels all the way back to the settlements. Two of the bronze cannons were abandoned along the way, to be displayed with pride by the victors for many years.

The following year, 1760, the Spanish patched up a truce with the Comanches and built two small missions nearer the settlements for the Lipans, but these missions soon failed. Under continuing Comanche attacks the Lipans gave way to the west and in a few years all of them had left Texas. The remnants of the tribe fled on across New Mexico and joined the other Apache bands already established in southeastern Arizona. Thus by the end of the eighteenth century only the Gataka Apaches and the Kiowa Apaches, both very small tribes, were left on the Plains of all the Apache migrations. Later the Gataka Apaches were dispersed and lost their identity, while the Kiowa Apaches, as allies of the powerful Kiowas, were safe from Comanche aggression and so survived to become one of the Plains tribes of the nineteenth century.

In 1763, at the close of the Seven Years' War, the Treaty of Paris transferred all of the French holdings west of the Mississippi and the city port of New Orleans to the Spanish. This gave the Spanish control of all the trade with the Plains tribes in the southern area. The Spanish immediately ordered the fur traders to stop at once all trading of guns and ammunition to the various Indian tribes, especially to the Comanches, but some of the French fur traders who remained in Louisiana ignored the Spanish orders and smuggled guns into the Red River country for another twenty years.

High-ranking Spanish officials believed that the Comanches could be of real value to Spain if they would keep any traders, either French or British, from entering the Plains from the east. For this reason these officials did not want Spanish soldiers to make any punitive raids against the Comanches in attempts to punish them for raids directed against the Spanish colonies in Texas and New Mexico. While this plan greatly reduced the military expenditures for the frontier posts of these colonies and thus saved the Spanish government a great deal of money over the years, the settlers along the borders bore the full cost of the Comanche raids, and this included the lives of many of their number as well as the loss of their livestock, crops, and homes.

In order to implement their policy, the officials ordered the governor in New Mexico to maintain friendly relations with the Comanches at all cost, and to allow them to trade freely at Taos. When the

Comanches staged an especially severe raid against the small settlements along the Pecos River, they aroused the ire of the governor to the extent that he sent his troops against the Comanches. For this action he was severely reprimanded by his superiors.

The working out of this policy is well illustrated by an incident in the summer of 1774.[6] Several Comanche raids over a short period of time in the Pecos Valley aroused the military commander, Carlos Fernandez, to take retaliatory action. He led a force of Spanish soldiers and Indian allies eastward into the Plains on the hot trail of one of the raiding bands. He managed to surprise the Comanche camp, for they were not expecting any soldiers, and killed or captured most of the people. When his report of this expedition reached Mexico City, they retorted with a blistering criticism and told him he had no reason to make such an attack on the Comanche allies, nor did Governor Mendinette at Santa Fe have the authority to allow such an action. The officials insisted that both the commander and the governor should have ignored the raid entirely. Then the Comanches would have brought the captives taken on the Pecos River into Taos for ransom and so would have been less angry at the Spanish than they were after losing some of their people in the fight.

Five years later New Mexico had a new governor.[7] At that time Spain was deeply involved in warring against Great Britain and the officials at Madrid could not keep as close a watch on the remote colony of New Mexico as they had been doing. The new governor, Don Juan Bautista de Anza, a good soldier who understood Indians and frontier conditions, decided he would forestall the next Comanche raid by striking them first. He had eighty-five good soldiers and soon found six hundred Ute warriors who were pleased at this opportunity to strike a blow at their enemies.

Anza made no attempt to reach the Comanche villages by the usual route from Taos across the mountain passes to the northeast. Instead he followed his Ute guides who led him by their old trail up the Rio Grande to the San Luis Valley, then eastward across the mountains by the old trails between the Ute and Comanche lands, much used when the two tribes were friends. No Spanish soldier had ever been in this backcountry. This roundabout march caught the Comanches completely by surprise and allowed the Spanish to reach a lightly defended village before the Indians had any warning of impending danger. Most of the men of the village had just gone off a few days before along the regular trail to make an attack on farms in the Taos area. This was the raid Anza had been expecting and he had strengthened the Taos defenses against it just before he left on his own expedition.

The war party against Taos was led by a famous Comanche leader, Green Horn, and it so happened that it was against Green Horn's home village that the first Spanish attack was launched. After Anza had wiped out the village, killing most of the people including women and children, as was the practice on both sides in this warfare, he laid a trap along the trail by which Green Horn and his men were expected to return. Those famous warriors had suffered a severe, unexpected repulse at Taos and were returning in low spirits when they rode right into the Spanish ambush where Green Horn, his eldest son, and a number of his important followers were killed along with several ordinary warriors.

Had Anza been allowed to continue on his aggressive program in New Mexico, he probably could have concluded a favorable peace with the Comanches in a year or two, but the Mexican officials refused to send him any more soldiers or any supplies for his small force. Instead the king gave him a new order to treat the Indians more kindly. This weak policy invited new Comanche attacks which were difficult for the settlers to beat off, for most of them were not permitted to own guns for the defense of their homes.

The brunt of the Comanche attacks was borne by the settlers in Texas to the north and west of San Antonio, and by those in New Mexico at Pecos and Taos. What particularly aroused the settlers in New Mexico was the practice, by order of the king, of allowing the Comanches to ride directly from their raids on Pecos to the market at Taos where they were welcomed and their captives, taken just a few days before on the last raid, were ransomed without any embarrassing questions being asked about when and where the people had been captured. The settlers were sure too that the Comanches would return for another attack on their farms within the next few months.

By 1780 the long, aggressive Comanche campaigns against their neighbors, particularly the Apaches, had given the tribe a claim to all the High Plains from the Nebraska border south into central Texas. The ramparts of the Rocky Mountains marked the western edge of their lands while on the east the Pawnees, Kansas, Osages, and Wichitas, all well supplied with guns, held the wild nomads at bay.

After their success against the San Saba mission, the Comanches found the way open to their raiding parties for dashes on to the south, where they harassed the settlers around San Antonio. They also continued to make their yearly trading visits to the Caddoan villages on the Red River where they bought their supplies of guns and ammunition. This contact finally brought them a great disaster.

In 1780 smallpox spread from the Spanish settlers at San Antonio northward to the Red River villages just in time for the Comanche trading parties to catch it. The disease then traveled northwest across the Plains, then northward near the mountains, passing from tribe to tribe until it reached even to the Crees, Assiniboins, and Blackfeet on the extreme northern edge of the Plains in Canada. There at the forests it stopped for want of victims to carry it farther.

The mortality among all the tribes attacked by the scourge was high, with each tribe losing about one half or more of its people. In some camps the entire group perished, leaving the tattered tipi coverings flapping in the wind and the whitened bones of people littering the ground for years to come. Skeletons of dogs were scattered all about, for those animals died horribly from feasting on the putrid corpses of their former masters. This widespread disaster had an important influence on the intertribal relationships throughout the Plains for the next thirty-five years.

7

Northern Plains Tribes
prior to 1780

WHILE THE COMANCHES WERE RAMPAGING through the southern Plains, plundering, slaughtering, and dispossessing other tribes as they enlarged their hunting grounds, the Shoshonis they had split from in southern Idaho on the upper Snake River were enjoying a long period of prosperity and growth with very little fighting. Buffalo herds had come from the Plains across the South Pass in recent years and had spread into the valleys of the Green and Bear rivers, while other herds had come up the Yellowstone Valley and had crossed the Bozeman Pass into the upper Missouri drainage which is composed of the valleys of the Gallatin, Madison, and Jefferson rivers and their tributaries. From the upper Madison Valley and the Beaverhead they had spread on to the south across the Continental Divide through several easy passes into the upper drainage of the Snake River in southeastern Idaho.

Once across the Continental Divide the buffalo spread out in all directions where they could find any good grazing. In a few years they had occupied all the grasslands that could support their small herds, but they left most of the Great Basin and all of the Snake River country west of American Falls empty. The desert scrub in those areas was as formidable a barrier to the grazing herds as a mountain wall, for even a small band of buffalo, feeding in a compact group as was their pattern, could not glean a subsistence from the little bunches of grass scattered among the shrubs, and the lack of water on the higher ranges was an added handicap to buffalo that were accustomed to go to their watering places at least once a day. Thus a map showing the areas occupied by buffalo west of the mountains would show great stretches of empty land off to the west, and unless it was a map that also showed the vegetation barrier there would be no apparent reason for the limited expansion of the herds.

To the south the buffalo followed down the valley of the Bear River to Great Salt Lake. They continued on south along the grasslands between the salt flats on the west and the steep, rugged mountain wall to the east. This brought them to the Sevier Valley where they found a pass across the Uinta Mountains and so reached the upper Colorado River country, but they were too few in number to establish themselves in this new land and were wiped out by the Utes.

The Shoshonis in the upper Snake country secured their horses from the Utes, surely as early as 1690, for by 1710 they owned large herds, raising the animals in substantial numbers in a large area well suited to range horses. They supplied themselves, their neighbors to the immediate west, the Bannocks, and the Shoshonis yet farther west on the Boise and Payette rivers. The Flatheads from the Bitterroot Valley in western Montana crossed the mountains on a visit and sneaked back with their first horse, a very tame mare they stole on a dark night from a herd grazing near a Shoshoni camp. Later they secured other horses through trade and some more theft and settled down to raising their own horses. The Shoshonis in the Boise area traded some horses to both the Cayuses and the Nez Percés as early as 1720.

After the Shoshonis in the upper Snake country were well mounted and had learned to hunt buffalo by practicing on their small herds, they expanded their hunting activities across the Continental Divide on the headwaters of the Missouri where other Shoshonis lived. Here the Shoshoni activities brought them into conflict with the Kiowas who then held the Gallatin and Madison valleys south of Three Forks. There may have been some fighting between the two tribes, for the Kiowas soon packed up and left the Missouri country. They crossed Bozeman Pass and went on down the Yellowstone where they joined the small tribe of Kiowa Apaches who had lagged behind the main Apache migration about two centuries earlier. From this time on the Kiowas and Kiowa Apaches acted more like a single tribe, living and hunting together and presenting a united front against all their foes.

These two tribes did not tarry along the Yellowstone. At that time the Wind River Shoshonis had moved into their permanent homeland just to the south of the Yellowstone Valley, and the Crows were living on the lower Yellowstone, probably as far upstream as Sidney and Glendive. The Kiowas turned south up the Powder River Valley, then moved off to the east and spread out along the northern slopes of the Black Hills, at that time empty of other humans. There they remained for about half a century.

After the Kiowas had left the Gallatin Valley, the Shoshoni mounted bands followed along their trail into Yellowstone Valley, then turned north and hunted buffalo on the open Plains just east of the Crazy Mountains. The Shoshonis considered this part of the Montana Plains as their own hunting grounds until the last buffalo were killed off there about 1880. There was a period from about 1810 until 1837 when the Blackfeet kept the Shoshonis to the west of the mountains for most of the time, but they returned to the Plains at every opportunity.

The Shoshonis on the upper Missouri traded horses to their brethren who occupied extensive holdings around Great Falls and up Sun River to the west. They in turn passed some of the animals along to the northernmost Shoshonis, a band then living in Alberta along the Bow River. The Blackfeet reported that they had heard of these Shoshonis having horses as early as the 1720s. They were a rugged people and fierce fighters and held the Blackfeet at bay along the line of Red Deer River, well to the north of Bow River, until they were seriously weakened by the smallpox epidemic of 1780.

If the Shoshoni traditions are to be believed, the Wind River Shoshonis in central Wyoming were the last of all the several Shoshoni divisions to get horses. The Wind River Shoshonis claimed that they had their first animals from the Comanches to the south in Kansas about 1740. It is probable that the tradition is wrong, like the Blackfoot tradition that their first horses came from the Nez Percés when in fact they never met any of the Nez Percés until about sixty or seventy years after they definitely had horses.

The Wind River Shoshoni had a very easy summer trail to the west into Green River Valley, Bear River Valley, and on down the Portneuf River to the upper Snake River country. It seems probable that they had some trade and cultural contacts with the Shoshonis who often hunted on Bear River, and who had horses at least as early as

1690, about ten years before the Comanches secured their first horses from the Utes. In considering these facts, it seems obvious that the Wind River Shoshoni visited their fellow tribesmen who had horses and so should have secured some of the animals for themselves, about twenty-five or thirty years before they could possibly have had any from the Comanches. This is another case in which the traditions are at fault in some details.

During all this period, while the western half of the Plains was undergoing several important changes, the southeastern border was stable although there was much activity among the tribes there. Along the Arkansas and Red rivers the Wichitas and southern Pawnees kept a firm grip on the gun trade out of New Orleans. By keeping themselves well armed and alert, and by supplying a good trading center where the Comanches could always dispose of their surplus horses for guns, these two tribes were able to maintain peaceful relations with the nomadic raiders. They also repelled all attempted advances toward the buffalo country by the woodland tribes just to the east. North of the Wichitas the powerful, well-armed Osages held their home villages and farmlands while they extended their buffalo hunting farther out into the Plains to the west.

The Dakotas who had held a large segment of the Minnesota lake country for two centuries or more had by now increased until by 1600 there were several thousand of them living in many small villages scattered about among the lakes and swamps. They had substantial frame houses covered with large slabs of bark, and their wild rice fields in the swamps and along the borders of the lakes furnished them a good grain crop each year without their having to do anything more than harvest the rice as it ripened. Their meat supply came from the deer in the woods and the buffalo herds in the open glades among the scattered groves of trees to the west. As their population grew, they were forced to build new villages toward the west to accommodate the extra people, and to depend more on the buffalo herds for meat.

Then about the middle of the seventeenth century the Crees along the Great Lakes secured guns from the French fur traders and at once began using their new weapons to enlarge their trapping grounds to the west, in order to secure more furs to trade for French goods. They also seemed to have a lust for fighting and made many of their raids just to kill people. Soon the westward thrust of these forest Indians was felt in some of the small villages on the eastern rim of the Dakota holdings.

The inhabitants abandoned their villages and moved on to the west, but the lake country there was fully occupied by other Dakota bands to the edge of the Plains. These fugitives were forced to go out beyond the forest edge and into the Plains before they could find any room to build new villages for themselves. Fortunately for them, there were a few scattered groves of trees and a good supply of drinking water in the area, but they were well beyond the edge of the rice growing country so they of necessity had to become seminomadic buffalo hunters if they were to survive.

By 1700 some of the Teton and Oglala bands of the Dakotas were spending more than half of each year on their long hunting trips. Since they had no crops to tend or harvest they did not need to return in August as did so many of the seminomadic tribes. These bands returned to their villages only for the winter months when they needed the extra shelter of their lodges and their small grove of trees as well as the additional supply of fuel the groves provided. Since they had no wild rice swamps, when they needed grain to tide them over the winter they traded off dried buffalo meat and robes to the sedentary Dakota bands for the necessary grain.

About 1760 small bands of Dakotas hunting to the southwest along the lower James River secured their first horses, probably from the Arickaras. Up to this time the Arickaras had considered them rather poverty stricken. When a small Teton band first appeared at the Arickara villages they were poorly clad and had almost no food supplies to carry them through the impending winter, for this was in mid-November and the weather was bleak and cheerless. They begged enough corn from the Arickaras for the winter months.

The prosperous, well-fed Arickaras looked out of their strongly fortified village at these ragged wanderers and formed a poor opinion of them. Although they gave them some help and allowed them to camp near by for a time, they made no offers of friendship. At that time the Tetons had no horses while the Arickaras had plenty for their buffalo hunting, and it is probable that the Tetons were able to trade a horse or two the first time they had a good hunting year and had dried meat and robes to offer the Arickaras.

The various Dakota bands continued to secure horses from the southwest in fairly large numbers for at the end of ten more years all the Dakota villages were credited with owning a few of the animals, but even the nomadic bands had too few for their needs. Here with a large tribe of about twenty-five thousand to supply with animals, even when the horse population had increased to several thousand head, the individual bands still had very few and most of the families in the nomadic bands had to be satisfied with one pack horse for each family. The Dakotas were so far from the source of supply in the Spanish colonies in New Mexico, and the expanding horse frontier at that time stretched from Minnesota to the Canadian Rockies, that even the acquisition of several thousand horses caused very little movement of the frontier.

The Arickaras at that period were rich and powerful compared to the much more numerous Dakotas and were able to hold their lands along the Missouri against all attacks, even after the Dakotas were able to secure ample supplies of guns. Although the Arickaras lost very heavily in the smallpox epidemic they were able to live securely behind their village walls until 1837.

After the Dakotas secured a good supply of horses they speeded up their movement out into the Plains. By 1780 they had advanced their western boundary nearly to the Missouri River and had taken over control of a wide belt of buffalo country in the eastern part of both South and North Dakota. All of the Indian bands in this whole expanse were either Tetons or Oglalas, with possibly a few Brulés here and there. In all they comprised about two-fifths of the entire Dakota tribe. The remaining three-fifths, usually called the Santee group, still stayed firmly settled in the Minnesota lake country. As the population of the Santee group increased, some of them moved out to the west and occupied the village sites left vacant by the Teton and Oglala bands that had become entirely nomadic by this time. These Santee Dakotas continued to hold onto their own homes for about another century, until they were finally driven out by the soldiers in 1862.

The Cheyennes, a tribe of the Algonkin stock, probably lived for a long period in farming villages near the south shore of Lake Erie until that area became overcrowded. Then they migrated to the west, probably in a series of easy stages, across northern Illinois and up the Mississippi. They finally found a pleasant valley suitable for farming on the lower Minnesota River and with no earlier settlers living there to dispute their possession. They then resumed their farming, building a series of small villages and putting in many small plots of corn, beans, and squash. They had fish from the streams and small lakes, and deer from the woodlands, but they depended on the small bands of buffalo pasturing in the glades and meadows for their major source of meat.

At some period during their westward progress, probably soon after they crossed the Mississippi, the tribe had split into two groups, with the smaller portion, known as the Sutaios, going directly west across the Plains to the Missouri River. There they found a long stretch of the valley unoccupied, illustrating again the emptiness of the Plains, and even of the major river valleys, until the middle of the seventeenth century.

Here on the Missouri, about on the border between North and South Dakota, the Sutaios built their little villages of earth lodges and planted their usual crops. Upriver to the north were the Mandan villages, too far away to be of any danger, and far down the river in Nebraska were the Pawnees, for the other valley tribes, including the Arickaras, had not yet arrived.

After a century or so the Cheyennes in the Minnesota valley found themselves the indirect victims of the expanding French fur trade. About 1650 French traders working along the western shore of Lake Michigan began selling guns and ammunition to the Ojibways and Winnebagos in order to increase the take of furs by those tribes. The Indians then expanded their trapping areas to the west across Wisconsin, at first keeping to the south of the numerous Dakota villages among the lakes and swamps. They began a long series of sporadic attacks on the Cheyenne villages that in time forced those farmer folk to again abandon their settlements and move off to the northwest where they resumed their farming around Lake Traverse on the Minnesota-Dakota border. It was during this stay at Lake Traverse that the Cheyennes secured their first horses and so made themselves more proficient buffalo hunters. This increase in the meat supply made them less dependent on their corn crops for winter food.

As the Ojibways and Winnebagos continued to push on to the west into the Minnesota lake country, they drove some of the small Dakota villages out and forced them to move farther toward the Dakota border and thus brought increased pressure on the Cheyennes, for these new Dakota village sites encroached on the Cheyenne holdings. The Cheyennes were too few in number to resist the numerous Dakotas and packed up to move to new lands.

About half the Cheyennes then decided to go off to the southwest across the open Plains to the Missouri and join the Sutaios. There is a tradition that the Sutaios at first resisted them and there was some friction for a short time between the new arrivals and the older settlers, but this was soon resolved and the two groups became a single tribe in a few years with the Sutaios having a definite segment of the tribal circle set aside for them when the whole tribe met. In a few years the population of the combined groups grew to such an extent they felt crowded. They could not send part of the tribe downriver, for by this time the Arickaras had moved in from Nebraska. Finally a large number of the Cheyennes moved across the Missouri and built homes a few miles to the west up the tributary streams. Most of these were Sutaios and so led some observers to believe that the Cheyennes had driven them out of the river valley. However, the whole group was still closely united and they remained in these villages until the opening of the nineteenth century.

The other portion of the Cheyenne tribe moved from Lake Traverse to the Sheyenne River of North Dakota. There on the southern loop of the river they found a wide valley empty of people, and with good farming land and some timber. For better defense against possible future enemies they put all their lodges in one village on a bluff above the river and strongly fortified it with a deep ditch and a palisade.

For several years they enjoyed a pleasant life in this new location. The farmland was fertile and their crops grew well. They gradually built up their horse herd until they had about one horse for each family, plenty for buffalo hunting, but far too few for a tribe of nomads so they had no incentive to leave their village and go wandering. The buffalo ranged for a large part of each year just to the west and south of town, so the Cheyenne hunters seldom had to go more than a day's journey from home for their meat. At first enemy raiders were far away, but they were inching closer each year.

8

The Plains Indians in 1780

T HE YEAR 1 7 8 0 was arbitrarily chosen by James Mooney of the
American Bureau of Ethnology for his estimates of the sizes of all the
different Plains tribes. At that time none of these tribes had been
greatly influenced by the westward-moving white settlers, although
some of the European culture items, particularly the gun and the horse,
had caused far-reaching and permanent changes among all of these
tribes.

In 1780 the entire Plains area seemed to be in a fairly stable
condition. All of the tribes by then had acquired horses and had put
them to use both in hunting buffalo and as pack animals. They had
adjusted their patterns of living somewhat to take advantage of these
new servants, and except for the Comanches, none of them were
engaged in intertribal warfare on a large scale.

In the following year, 1781, a smallpox epidemic wiped out about
half of the entire population of all the Plains tribes, estimated in 1780 at
about 130,000 people. This disaster was sudden, widespread, and
covered all the tribes. When it was over the various tribes had to begin
a new era of development.

By 1780 all the Plains tribes had become seminomadic or nomadic,
and each of them had established claims to a large hunting area around
the home villages or favorite camping spots. All of the Plains except for

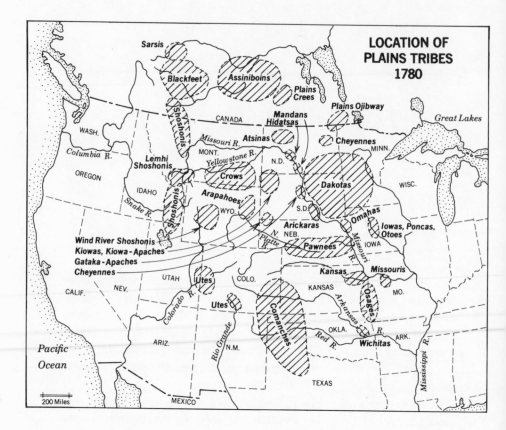

a few rather narrow buffer strips, and the large triangle of land between the Missouri and Yellowstone rivers, had been divided up among the various claimants.

The year 1780 then marks the end of an era, and is a good point to end a summary of the early period of the Plains tribes. Here is a brief summary of the movements of each tribe, its location in 1780, and its strength. Thus, the stage will be set for the great cultural changes of the next century, and for the long period of intertribal warfare that accompanied the changes. These summaries are arranged more by geographical areas, than by language groups.

Down on the southeastern corner of the Plains were the Wichitas, a tribe of Caddoan stock that had come north from eastern Texas in the fourteenth century to settle along the Great Bend of the Arkansas. During the eighteenth century they moved downriver into Oklahoma. They secured their first horses about 1680. Estimated population in 1780 was 3,000.

Just to the north of the Wichitas, in western Missouri, were the Osages, a Siouan tribe from southern Indiana. They had moved west about 1650, and secured horses by 1700. Estimated population in 1780 was 6,200.

Just north of the Osages on the south bank of the Missouri were the Missouris, a Siouan tribe from northern Illinois. They too had moved west about 1650, and had horses by 1730. Their estimated population in 1780 was 1,200.

On the west side of the Missouri in the Kaw Valley were the Kansas, also of Siouan stock, who had come west from the Ohio Valley with the Osages about 1650. They secured horses in 1724. Estimated population in 1780 was 3,300.

On the west side of the Missouri in the Platte Valley and some adjoining territory were the Pawnees, a Caddoan tribe that had come to the Plains in two migrations, one from east Texas in the thirteenth century the other from the upper Ohio Valley about 1650. They secured horses about 1720. Estimated population in 1780 was 10,000.

On up the Missouri, at about the Nebraska-South Dakota border, were the Omahas, another Siouan tribe that came west with the Osages and finally reached the Missouri about 1690. They secured horses about 1730. Estimated population in 1780 was 2,800.

Neighbors to the Omahas were three small, closely related tribes of Siouan stock, the Iowas, Otoes, and Poncas. They had come from southern Wisconsin into Iowa possibly by 1600 and had moved several times about the state. They secured horses about 1730. Estimated populations in 1780: Iowas—1,100; Otoes—900; Poncas—800.

The Cheyennes, of Algonkin stock, were split into two groups in 1780, one on the Missouri River about at the South Dakota-North Dakota line, the other on the Sheyenne River in North Dakota. They had come originally from south of Lake Erie and settled in the Minnesota River Valley. Then they split, one group going west to the

Missouri, the other via Lake Traverse to the Sheyenne River. They secured horses about 1750. Estimated population in 1780 was 3,500 total for both groups.

The Dakotas, the largest of the Plains tribes, were of Siouan stock. They came originally from the Ohio Valley and may have spent several hundred years in the Wisconsin and Minnesota country before about half of them moved onto the Plains late in the eighteenth century. By 1780 they held a large portion of western Minnesota and most of the eastern half of the Dakotas. They secured their first horses about 1750. Estimated population in 1780 was 27,000.

To the north of the Dakotas in the Red River Valley in Manitoba were the Plains Ojibways of Algonkin stock, who had emerged from the forests to the northeast about 1690. They had horses about 1770. Estimated population in 1780 was 3,000.

Just to the west of the Plains Ojibways were the Plains Crees along the Saskatchewan River. They also were of Algonkin stock and had come out of the forests about 1690. They had horses by 1770. Estimated population in 1780 was 4,000.

To the southwest of the Plains Crees along the Canadian border were the Assiniboins of Siouan stock. They had come from the Ohio Valley as a part of the Dakotas and had broken away to move on to the northwest possibly by 1600. The Plains Crees had forced them on to the west about 1690, then the two tribes became allies. They secured horses in the 1730s. Estimated population in 1780 was 10,000.

Off to the northwest in northern Alberta were the Blackfeet, of Algonkin stock. They had moved west from the forests near Hudson's Bay about 1680, and secured horses by the 1730s. Their estimated population in 1780 was 5,000.

Just to the north of the Blackfeet were the Sarsis, of Athapascan stock. They secured horses from the Blackfeet about 1760. Estimated population in 1780 was 700.

In 1780 southern Alberta and north central Montana were held by a strong group of Shoshonis who were driven from the Plains by 1785 and so never became one of the Plains tribes.

On the Missouri River in South Dakota, just to the north of the Omahas, were the Arickaras, of Caddoan stock, who had recently split from the Pawnees. They had horses about 1740. Estimated population in 1780 was 3,800.

Above the Arickaras on the Missouri were half of the Cheyennes, mentioned previously. Above them were the Mandans, of Siouan stock, who had come from the Ohio Valley and across the Mississippi before 1500. They had horses about 1745. Estimated population in 1780 was 3,600.

On up the Missouri several miles above the Mandans were the Hidatsas, also of Siouan stock. They had been driven from the Red River Valley by the Plains Ojibways and had moved across to the Missouri about 1700. Estimated population in 1780 was 2,500.

On the High Plains to the northwest of the Hidatsa and Mandan villages were the Atsinas, of Algonkin stock. They had come out of the forests into the Saskatchewan Valley and had been driven from there about 1700. They secured horses about 1750. Estimated population in 1780 was 3,000.

On the Yellowstone fork of the Missouri the Crows held the land from Powder River on west to Big Horn River. They were of Siouan stock, and had separated from the Hidatsas on the Missouri about 1700 and had moved on upstream by easy stages. They secured horses about 1730. Estimated population in 1780 was 4,000.

On the upper Powder River were the Arapahoes of Algonkin stock, who had separated from the Atsinas in North Dakota about 1700. They had horses by 1730, or a little earlier. Estimated population in 1780 was 3,000.

The country in South Dakota just north of the Black Hills was held by the Kiowas, very distant relations to the Shoshonis. They may have come up from Arizona by 1200 and had lived in southwestern Montana until about 1720, when they moved down the Yellowstone and on over to the Black Hills. They had horses about 1730. Estimated population in 1780 was 2,000.

With the Kiowas were the Kiowa Apaches that had come from northern Canada to the Yellowstone by 1600, and had joined the Kiowas on their trek east. Estimated population in 1780 was 500.

In the southern Colorado mountain valleys and on the Colorado River drainage in western Colorado were the Utes, of Shoshoni stock, whose ancestors had come from southern Arizona by way of Virgin River into the eastern Utah-western Colorado country by 1300. They had horses about 1660. Estimated population in 1780 was 4,500.

The circle of the Plains is completed with the Comanches, of Shoshoni stock, who had come from southern Arizona by way of the Virgin River, Sevier River, Bear River, and Yampa River into the

Colorado mountains. As soon as they secured horses, about 1700, they moved out onto the Plains. By 1780 they held most of eastern Colorado, western Kansas, western Oklahoma, and a large part of northern Texas. Estimated population in 1780 was 12,000.

9

Smallpox: The Scourge of the Plains

SMALLPOX WAS THE DEADLIEST of all the diseases, in terms of the number of people killed, that were brought to North America from Europe and turned loose among the primitive people of the New World. It was most active among the Plains tribes in the period 1781–1838, and wrought many drastic changes among the buffalo-hunting tribes, especially those in the Northwest. On these primitive people the attack of this dread disease was sudden, unheralded, and very deadly. It swept through the tribes at great speed, wiping out entire villages, killing half or more of each tribe, and bringing about new intertribal relationships and adjustments.

Europeans, from centuries of experience with the pox, knew that it was both contagious and infectious. Not only could a person catch it directly from the victim days before the eruptions came on the skin but it could also be acquired by coming in contact with clothing and blankets used by the sick, sometimes even months after the patients had died. The Indians could not grasp the idea of infection or contagion, and refused to take the protective measures advised by the white men who tried to protect them.

Once smallpox reached an Indian camp or village it spread rapidly to everybody, for the Indians had no conception of the principles of quarantine. Indians from other tribes who came to the stricken village to trade, or those small bands of enemy raiders lurking about ready to lift a scalp or two even from an invalid dying of the disease, carried away the germs unknowingly, so that even in the sparsely inhabited Plains and western mountains the plague was quickly dispersed over a wide area.

The great epidemic of 1780–81 began quietly enough with a few cases of the pox in San Antonio, where a major portion of the community was immune from having survived earlier attacks of the disease. When the Indians from the Caddoan villages to the north came to San Antonio for their annual trading, they caught the pox and carried it back to their villages on the Red River before they even realized that they were seriously ill.

On the Red River the pox was soon acquired by the Comanches when they came in to trade their spare horses for guns and ammunition, as they had been doing for years. The Comanches carried the disease all across the southern Plains and into New Mexico after they returned to their usual haunts. Some of the Comanches in southern Colorado started the pox northward along the foothills of the Rockies. It spread so rapidly along this old north-south trail that by the spring of 1781 it was on the upper Missouri. Never pausing, it went its deadly course until it reached the Canadian forests where it finally stopped for the want of new victims, but by then it had left a good half of all the Indians along the way dead in its wake.

Smallpox, like measles and scarlet fever, was always accompanied by a high fever. The Indian tribes often treated any feverish symptoms the same way they handled arthritis, stiff joints, or rheumatism—by a ritualistic steam bath designed to cleanse the body and purify the soul in one session. In a permanent village this sort of treatment was so common that a permanent sweat lodge was considered an essential structure. It was usually about five feet high, dome-shaped, and covered with a layer of earth. A heavy robe or hide was used to seal the entrance at the proper time. In a camp the lodge was made with bent willow poles covered with layers of hide.

Any person feeling the need for a steam bath came to this lodge, usually with a few friends. They built a fire outside near the entrance to heat rounded stones from the river. Rough stones from talus slopes or hills were never used as they might explode when they were heated and had cold water splashed on them.

When the stones were very hot they were moved into the sweat lodge and sprinkled with a little water "to clean grandfather's face" by rinsing off the ashes, but this was really a precaution to find out in time if any of these rocks might explode. Once the stones were clean, the group entered the lodge, someone on the outside completely sealed the entrance and more water was sprinkled on the hot stones. Often an appropriate chant accompanied the steaming process.

After a few minutes the group threw back the robe over the entrance and they all dashed for the nearby stream where they plunged into the cold water. While this steaming did thoroughly cleanse the body and often relieved aches and pains, it was definitely the wrong treatment for smallpox and usually brought a quick, painful death to the feverish patient. This steam bath-cold plunge treatment might well have doubled the fatalities among the Plains tribes.

The nomadic life pattern of the hunting tribes in the summer months also added to the deadliness of the epidemic diseases. An Indian camp was crammed with people, horses, and dogs, and there were no provisions for disposing of the refuse and excrement. In the Plains under normal conditions this accumulation of filth was no great problem. Instead of trying to keep a camp clean, the Indians found it much easier and simpler just to move to a new, clean campsite every day or two. They explained that the Great Spirit became angry with his people if they camped too long in one spot and sent flies and plagues as a punishment if they lingered more than a day or two.

But when a disease such as the smallpox struck and each tipi had its quota of fever victims, moving was impossible. The campsite rapidly became foul with swarms of flies breeding in every pile of refuse, then carrying the various kinds of infection to everyone through their food. In extreme cases every person in the camp or village perished, leaving their tattered tipi coverings flapping in the breeze, their horse herds scattered, and their putrid bodies to be devoured by the hungry dogs that soon perished from their unwholesome diet.

Enemy scouts who found such a stricken camp had their choice of the horse herds. Then hoping for a scalp or two they usually skulked around at dusk, looking for some poor old woman out for a few sticks of wood or some drinking water, but her scalp could be counted at full value for it had been taken from an enemy. Then the raiders rode home with their loot, totally unaware that they were also carrying the germs of the dread pox to their people, probably in the scalp of the poor old woman.

Thus by trading parties or enemy raiders the pox traveled from the Caddoan villages to the Comanches, to the Arapahoes, to the Crows, to the Assiniboins, and finally to the Plains Crees on the Saskatchewan River. Losses were very heavy among the Assiniboins and Crees, but probably no heavier than those of the Arapahoes and Crows. From the Canadian tribes the fur traders had firsthand accounts of the fatalities in their trading areas and reported the figures to their superiors where they became a matter of record while the thousands of Arapahoes and Crows died unrecorded by white men.

The Crows also passed the pox along to their neighbors to the northwest, the Shoshonis on Sun River in Montana who sent it along to their brethren along the Bow River in Alberta. They in turn gave it to their neighbors who were also their bitterest enemies, the Blackfeet, who lost about a third of their people. It is possible that the lower losses for the Blackfeet were due to their being scattered out in many small bands and some of the outlying bands may have escaped unscathed. The story of the pox among the Blackfeet came from a series of related incidents and the developments that followed.

When the Blackfeet moved west through the forest until they emerged in northern Alberta, they soon made friends with the Assiniboins, the neighboring tribe just to the southeast, who had arrived on the Plains in Saskatchewan some years earlier. The two tribes continued their friendly relations for many years and became such good neighbors that warriors from one tribe would often join war parties being organized by the other tribe. Particularly the Assiniboins, who were much the stronger at this early period, sent warriors to help the Piegans hold back the thrusts of the powerful Shoshoni bands that held most of Alberta in 1730 and who had recently acquired some horses from the Shoshonis who lived on the upper Missouri in southwestern Montana.

The Blackfeet were divided into three groups: the Piegans who guarded the southern border, the Bloods who had charge of watching the western mountain passes, and the Northern Blackfeet who had no special fighting assignments. Often though when the Piegans to the south needed some extra help against the Shoshonis, they found it easier to secure from the neighboring Assiniboins than from the other

Blackfoot bands. An added factor was that the Assiniboins had begun to buy guns from the French traders through their friends, the Plains Crees, who had given up their aggressions against the Assiniboins after a series of fights lasting for several years.

When the Shoshonis along the Bow River acquired their first horses, they expected that the animals would give them a great advantage over the Blackfeet in their next fight, but fortunately for the Blackfeet they were able to offset the Shoshoni horses with a few guns from the Assiniboins. With their new weapons and a few Assiniboin volunteers, the Piegan warriors marched off to the south and after some heavy fighting were able to push the Shoshonis across Red Deer River, which then remained the boundary between the two tribes until after the smallpox epidemic—a span of about fifty years.

The first knowledge of the presence of this dread disease in Alberta came to the Blackfeet through the Shoshonis who passed both the knowledge and the disease along unintentionally. Seven years after the event, while the details were still fresh in the mind of a survivor, the whole episode was related to David Thompson, a fur trader who visited the tribe with a large supply of trade goods from the Hudson's Bay Company.[1]

The Blackfoot warrior, a member of the Piegan band, explained that in order to defend themselves against surprise raids by the large and powerful group of Shoshonis who held the Bow River Valley in force, the Piegan band that lived just to the north of the Red Deer River, the frontier line between the two tribes and fifty miles to the northeast of the Shoshoni camps, regularly sent out scouting parties into the buffer strip to the south. Their chief duty was to watch for any Shoshoni hunters or scouts, and to check the Shoshoni camps for any signs of unusual activity, such as a large ceremonial dance that might presage a raid by a large war party.

In the summer of 1781, after the Shoshonis had been unusually quiet for a long time, the Piegan scouts worked their way carefully through an empty land until they reached the Bow River. There in a large meadow on the south bank they found a large Shoshoni camp with about a hundred tipis all arranged neatly in a large camp circle, and a small herd of horses grazing nearby, but the whole scene had a rather unnatural look, for there were no people to be seen anywhere and some small bands of buffalo were grazing peacefully with the horses. The scouts decided that the camp had been set up as a bait to invite a Blackfoot attack. Once the enemy had charged into the camp circle a large party of Shoshonis hidden in ambush would ride in and wipe out the attackers.

The wary scouts spent a day or two carefully studying the whole surrounding country. They worked their way off to the south for twenty miles or more, looking for any forces that might be preparing to move in for an ambush, but they found nothing. The whole land was empty. Finally they decided that they should make a surprise attack at dawn. Just at daybreak they came dashing up to the tipis, slashing at the leather coverings and whooping and yelling to further confuse and frighten the sleeping inmates as they struggled from their robes to face imminent destruction, but no Shoshonis even stirred in that camp of death. The tipi floors were littered with the bodies of smallpox victims, in all stages of decay. The few Shoshoni who had still been alive had left during the night, slipping away to the south under the cover of darkness. They had seen the scouts skulking about and had fled to their kinsmen far to the south.

The putrid Shoshoni dead were so gruesome that the scouts made no attempt to take any scalps. They did take several of the best tipi covers and some of the camp gear and personal belongings that seemed clean. They apparently limited their loot to what the Shoshoni horses could carry, for they rounded up the small herd, packed the animals with the plunder, and went home.

Shortly after they reached their own camp, the scouts began to sicken with the fever. In a few days they had infected all their families and friends. The Piegans had no idea that they had carried the disease back from the Shoshoni camp. The narrator told Thompson, "We had no belief that one man could give it to another any more than a wounded man could give his wound to another."

Luckily the Piegan camp was near a small, shallow stream, large enough to supply the small camp with drinking water but too small for the sweat bathers to plunge into, and only about a third of the people died. In other camps where the fever victims had a large, cold stream at hand, plunges by people burning with fever caused a very high mortality rate.

The Piegans were so dejected at their misfortune, believing that they were being punished by the Great Spirit for their past misdeeds,

". . . we thought of war no more and perhaps would have made peace with them [the Shoshoni] for they had suffered dreadfully as well as us and had left all this fine country of the Bow River to us." This statement clearly shows that the Blackfeet moved from the north bank of the Red Deer River to the Bow River just after 1781.

10

Horse Culture among the Plains Tribes

WHEN THE SMALLPOX EPIDEMIC HAD RUN its course, the remnants of the Plains tribes needed a period of a few years to reorganize their various bands, often combining the few survivors from two or three bands into one until their numbers built up again. But in spite of all their hardships and losses that summer, after their first winter they enjoyed a period of comparative prosperity and growth that lasted for about fifty years, and some of their better living conditions in this period stemmed directly from the sudden increase in the number of horses available to each survivor for immediate use. The sudden death of at least half the total population, with no corresponding loss of horses, left most of the tribes with herds ample for their needs. This increase was especially noticeable among those northern tribes that had been so slow in building up their herds and were still short of working animals in 1780.

The deaths of many of the owners of large herds throughout the entire Plains area brought a good deal of adjustment. Large bands of horses, set free by the deaths of their owners, ranged freely on the open plains until the survivors of the epidemic built up enough strength to round them up again. Thus the death of one wealthy Indian might scatter his horses among a dozen or more needy families and bring about a rapid redistribution of wealth that brought much easier living conditions to the lucky recipients of the unexpected bounty.

For a year or two another factor that kept the Plains more peaceful was the abrupt decrease in horse stealing. From late summer of 1781 until well through the next summer the survivors were much too busy in just staying alive and in replacing their stores of dried meat, robes, and tipi covers to take time for such relaxing activities as raiding the horse herds of tribes a few hundred miles away, and they had little incentive to strive very hard for more horses until they became more accustomed to their recent accession. They had lost a full season of hunting during their sickness, and had subsisted almost entirely on their food reserves. They did not regain an adequate reserve supply of dried meat and robes until after the summer hunt the following year.

It may come as a surprise to sedentary people to learn that a tribe could double its horses per person and still need more. Nomadic tribes living in Africa and Asia seemed to manage without such a large number of horses to ride and to carry their packs. Here the difference is that those tribes secured most of their food directly from their flocks and herds, animals that did not need to be hunted down each day. Sheep, goats, and cattle carried the meat supplies on the hoof until they were needed and so reduced the number of pack animals needed.

This need of the nomadic Indian for several horses can be illustrated by considering the life of the basic group in a hunting band, the people who lived in one lodge or tipi. In most of the Plains tribes about five to eight people could live in one tipi, although in some tribes, such as the Crows, who had an abundance of long, slender lodge poles, a tipi might be made large enough to hold up to twelve. The family in the usual tipi were one adult male, one or two women, and some children of various ages. Adequate transportation for such a group on the open plains, always on the move to fresh pastures for the horses, fresh camp grounds for the people, and fresh buffalo herds to hunt, had to take care of all the people and all of their worldly goods, including their portable shelter.

Each of the people needed a horse to ride, while the man needed a buffalo runner and a war horse in addition, seven to ten riding horses in all. Then to carry the tipi cover weighing about 250 pounds, drag a dozen or more long tipi poles, and to carry the clothing, sleeping robes, camp gear, and a little spare food required on the average of one pack horse per person, a minimum of five pack animals. This estimate is based on the common practice of having each of the mounts that carried a child carry a full pack load. Then the group would own three to five colts and yearlings too young to carry burdens. Hence the old-time trappers and traders in the West in estimating the number of people in an Indian camp or the size of the horse herd just counted the number of tipis, which would also give the number of warriors. Five times that number would give the approximate size of the band, and for a wealthy tribe, fifteen times that number would give the size of the horse herd. Wealthy tribes with adequate numbers of horses were the Comanches of the southern Plains, the Crows along the Yellowstone, and the Nez Percés, a Columbia Basin tribe that often hunted buffalo in Montana. Some tribes were so poor that they had to get along with only one or two horses for each tipi. They had a great deal of difficulty in moving camp and in hunting buffalo. Often they had to move camp in two stages with all of the horses and most of the people overburdened with packs on both trips from the old camp to the new.

When a nomadic band was moving across country, its general prosperity, and hence its ability to buy trade goods, could be assessed quickly by observing the women in any one small group. If all were riding, the band was wealthy and had a large horse herd, with a number of animals to be traded to the visitor for his goods. If some of the women were walking and leading pack horses, and many of the dogs were carrying packs or pulling small travois, the horse supply was scanty or the people were returning from a successful buffalo hunt with a temporary surplus of meat and hides. If many of the women were carrying packs, and the pack string included about two dogs for each horse, the band was quite poor in horses and probably had little worth trading. For some bands this might be just a temporary state resulting from a successful enemy raid that the men had not been able to offset yet by a similar raid of their own.

For about half of the Plains tribes this shortage of horses was the usual state. These were usually the seminomadic tribes, living through the winter in their permanent villages along the rivers, usually with a lack of good pasture near the villages. Usually too, such a tribe had no natural barriers around their pastures and lived rather near other tribes. This combination left their herds exposed to enemy raiders. In contrast, the Crows had a broad expanse of good pasture land between the Yellowstone River and the Big Horn Mountains, both good natural barriers, and across the Yellowstone there stretched a hundred miles or more of open country that offered little cover for raiding parties.

The shortage of horses among the have-not tribes cut down on their freedom of movement and reduced the efficiency of their hunting. This in turn kept them at a lower level of prosperity and rather effectually blocked their efforts toward bettering their condition. They always looked poverty-stricken to the explorers and fur traders even though they had much more food and clothing than they had possessed in the prehorse days. They entirely lacked that standard item of trade on the Plains, the extra horse.

Among the tribes with a surplus of horses, many of those animals were traded off each year for the white man's goods. Such surplus animals usually came from the large herds owned by wealthy individuals, and were just average pack animals, stallions or geldings, although some of the older mares might be traded. Tribes with horses to trade at almost any time were the Comanches, Crows, Kiowas, and Osages.

Although the Osages had less than half as many horses per person as the other tribes mentioned above, they had much less use for larger numbers, as they were short on winter pasture just as most of the seminomadic tribes were. Hence instead of holding their herds through the winter, sending them out onto the Plains under guard, they sold off or traded away many of the animals each fall, knowing that they could easily spare a portion of their trade goods in the spring to restock their herds in time for the summer hunt.

Although the Osages went on two extended buffalo hunts per year, they did not require as many horses per person as the true nomads. They left a portion of the tribe behind in the villages near the fields of growing crops to drive off the grazing animals and the birds. These people were the old, the crippled, and the very young. Then the Osages left a great deal of their property behind—tools, extra robes for winter, food reserves, and most of their fine costumes, for they had no need of such things in hunting buffalo, while the nomadic band had to take along everything it owned for it had no place to store the extra items.

When a prosperous nomadic band of about a hundred Indians was on the move, with a horse herd of a thousand or more animals, the horses could not be handled as one large herd. Instead each family unit took care of its own animals, keeping its riding horses, pack horses, and the loose young stock all in a fairly compact unit, separated from the other horses by a short distance, perhaps fifty to a hundred yards. Poor families, with only five or six horses each, often joined with close relatives to combine all their horses in one band for the march and they helped each other drive them.

Here is the account of such a band of Indians on the march along the Santa Fe Trail.[1] These were Cheyennes.

> Each lodge had its own band of horses, which presented a strange appearance; eighteen or more bands close to each other, walking along but not mixing; each band following a favorite mare, or perchance, a woebegone, scrawny mule, not worth the powder and ball to kill it. It is a strange and general fact that caballadas [horse herds] are mostly led by a no-account mare or mule—the greatest devil in the drove. They follow their erratic leader everywhere, like sheep, whether jumping, running, or grazing.

Horses like to live in small bands, following a chosen leader. This trait is very strong in all horses allowed to roam freely, either range herds or the wild horses. In the wilds or on the open range the leader is usually a stallion, although even there some wise old mare acts as the leader much of the time while the stallion mounts guard at a little distance, or brings up the rear, to nip the stragglers and to watch for any attack from that direction. In these Indian camps, each small group of animals is accustomed to follow a leader too, usually a wise old mare, for the mules in the Cheyenne herd are not often found in the eastern or northern Plains.

Only during times of great excitement will such a band break and scatter. Hence in the morning when the time comes to move camp, one of the young people, usually a teen-age boy, rides out and brings in his own band. If the pasture is good and the horses are grazing close by, the herder can walk up to the lead mare and ride her in. This pattern was very efficient and caused very little delay compared to the snorting, milling remuda at a cow camp, where each cowboy had to cut out and rope his mount for the day while it dashed around among a hundred others, for his saddle string never coalesced as a strongly knit group.

Until about 1800 there was a steady flow of horses each year from the Spanish settlements in the south toward the northern Plains as each succeeding tribe tried to secure an adequate supply of animals for its needs. As the tribes increased in numbers and the horses were used for more tasks, there was always a demand for more and more horses. At the same time the ranges along the Rio Grande in New Mexico became depleted and could no longer raise as many horses as the Indians wanted. For a time the Spanish ranches unwillingly helped with the supply, but first the Apaches, and later the Comanches, were forced to turn to the large stock ranches on the central plateau of Mexico to fill their needs.

The Indian raiders crossed the Rio Grande well down the river from El Paso and traveled up the Conchos River. On the upper drainage of the Conchos and across the divide in the central basin they found a wide expanse of open range filled with herds of horses and cattle so widely scattered that it was difficult for the Mexican stockmen and the soldiers to guard them from the wild warriors from the north. Each year the Mexican officials in the region reported staggering losses of horses, all driven off to the Plains, the estimate running to 100,000, 200,000, and even 500,000 a year.

That these estimates were grossly exaggerated is evident to anyone who has handled such records or who has worked with range stock and takes even a passing glance at the route down the Conchos and across the desert plateau north of the Rio Grande crossing. Even in very rainy seasons the pasturage along this route could not possibly accommodate more than about twenty thousand animals. And keep in mind that the raids usually took place in August under the full moon, the dreaded "Comanche Moon" of the Mexican victims. By that time of year the grass has been burned by the blazing sun and the water holes are few and far between.

Twenty thousand horses would eat up or trample down every blade of grass along the narrow Conchos Valley and leave nothing for any later herds. Other horses were brought across the Rio Grande well below the Big Bend country, but these came from other Mexican ranches east of the high plateau. On the lower river, from Laredo to Brownsville, horses could be taken across quite easily at any time except during the flood season. After 1830 more than half the Comanche raiding parties were following these lower trails and raiding deep into Mexico east of the mountains. Many of these raids were reported by the American soldiers posted in the small frontier forts after Texas gained its independence in 1836, and so loom large in the eyes of the historians, but these raids usually were on a smaller scale than those on the Conchos. A herd of a thousand rated a special report from the army posts.

It is possible that all the raids into Mexico brought in about 33,000 to 35,000 new animals each year. This would give for an average year 20,000 from the Conchos trail, possibly another thousand from New Mexico, and 12,000 from the lower Rio Grande. These new horses were spread out across the southern Plains from the Texas Panhandle to the Osage country in western Missouri within a few weeks after they reached the safety of the Plains.

One source, and quite an important one, of horses for the Plains tribes is frequently overlooked. This is the colt crop produced each year by the 75,000 to 100,000 mares owned by the various tribes. Stallions and geldings were more apt to be traded off, or to be lost in buffalo hunting and fighting so the herds commonly showed a majority of mares. Although in many tribes the colts were often neglected, enough of them survived to replace the usual deaths through accident, old age, and sickness. If it is common for a well-tended herd of range stock to produce an increase each year of 10 to 20 percent, it is not out of reason to expect the Indian herds to produce enough colts for replacements.

Another source for horses, and also apt to be overlooked, was the Columbia Basin. There several of the tribes produced a large number of colts each year above what they needed for replacements, and expected to trade off several hundred animals each summer. When the Nez Percés, Flatheads, Coeur d'Alenes, Spokanes, Yakimas, and, until 1855, the Cayuses, went across the Rocky Mountains each year to hunt buffalo, each hunting band customarily took several extra animals along for trading purposes. A traveler meeting one of these Nez Percé bands noted that their horses for trading were as numerous as the working horses, about three hundred head.

The many thousand horses stolen each year from the various tribes by raiders from other tribes need not be considered here, for these animals were not lost to the Plains area. They were merely passed from one tribe to another, and seldom did any one tribe suffer a large net loss of animals to thieves over a span of years, for their own young men were busy each year bringing in stolen horses to replace the losses. A glaring exception to this pattern is offered by the Lemhi Shoshonis, not classed as one of the Plains tribes. They lived in southern Idaho and suffered each year from thieves of the Plains tribes who came across the mountains raiding their herds. They had no tribe they could steal from, so they had to recoup their losses by raising more colts. It is obvious then that stolen horses became actual losses to the Plains area only when the animals were traded away to the settlers in the east, or, after 1850, to miners in the west.

Although the steady flow of horses from Mexico continued unabated after 1800, these animals no longer moved on north to the distant tribes. Most of these extra animals had been stolen by the Comanches and Kiowas, who then took them to the Caddoan villages along the Red River to be traded to the market in Louisiana, or to Natchez, where they were taken across the Mississippi and distributed through the southern states. The rest of the animals went north to the Osages who passed them along to St. Louis. From there they were taken across into Illinois and on to various markets in the Ohio Valley, with some of them even going east into the farming areas of Pennsylvania.

Although there is no way to check on the exact numbers of horses involved in this flow from the Plains tribes to the eastern farm markets, it would appear that the total outflow from the Plains approximated the influx of new stock from Mexico, New Mexico, and the Columbia Basin. Obviously then this trade did not produce any real shortage among the tribes on the southern Plains, for as early as 1800 there were thousands of wild horses, mustangs, there to be had for the catching. Although the tribes in that area did catch and tame a number of mustangs each year, they took only a small portion of the available animals, a strong indication that horses were not very scarce anywhere in the buffalo country in the nineteenth century.

11

The Plains Indians after 1780

Kiowas and Cheyennes

IN 1781, when the smallpox epidemic struck, the Kiowas were still living just north of the Black Hills. They suffered heavy losses to the disease although there is no contemporary report for them. Their total population is estimated to have dropped below two thousand, with not more than three hundred warriors. They gradually rebuilt their strength in the 1780s, and although they were still a rather small tribe, for some unaccountable reason they split into two groups. The larger section, possibly two thousand people, moved off to the south while the rest, about five hundred people, stayed behind with the Kiowa Apaches who were about five hundred strong at that time.

The southern trek of the main Kiowa band was through lands left almost empty by the smallpox. They crossed the Platte Valley just above the forks and went on south into western Kansas where they found very fine buffalo country. There they also found some bands of northern Comanches who had a combined strength of about two thousand people. These two groups then engaged in desultory conflict over a period of several years, with not very serious fighting at any time. Seemingly they raided each other more from a need for excitement than from any genuine enmity. Possibly the hostilities were confined almost entirely to horse stealing from one another.

Finally the two came together one summer in a big peace council and after several days of feasting they had eliminated all their points of friction and decided they should be friends. They then entered into a formal compact to be active allies, helping each other against common foes. This agreement involved about two thousand Kiowas and about the same number of Comanches. All of these events took place in western Kansas to the north of the Arkansas River and did not involve any of the southern Comanche bands in any way. It is doubtful that the Kiowas had even met any of the southern bands by this time.

This peace compact was never broken. The two groups shared a common hunting ground that was large enough for both, and cooperated in raids, especially into southern Texas. Although the Kiowas never made any formal agreement with the southern Comanches, there is no indication that there ever was serious friction between these two groups. The only times the two met were when the Kiowas went south to harry settlers around San Antonio, but most of this raiding took place much later, about the middle of the nineteenth century. The presence of these Kiowa raiders in southern Texas has led some writers to assume that the tribe moved its winter camps far to the south, but such was not the case. The Kiowas never considered any land south of Oklahoma as their home country, and they stayed north of the Arkansas River most of the period until 1840.

The combined bands of the northern Kiowas, and their neighbors, the Kiowa Apaches, numbered about 1,100 at the time of the split. They enjoyed a rather peaceful period of growth during the interval, 1785–1805, with no dangerous enemies close by. They were friendly with the Gataka Apaches just south of the Black Hills, who lived between the Pawnees to the east and the Arapahoes to the west. The Kiowas and the two Apache groups skirmished with their western neighbors, the Crows and Arapahoes, but they seem to have suffered very little from enemy war parties until the Teton Dakotas extended their raids in force west of the Missouri River after 1790, but they probably did not mount any serious attacks against the Kiowas even then.

Although the Tetons did not hunt out the Kiowas as far west as their camps, they did cause the Kiowas a great deal of trouble when the latter tried to go to the Arickara villages on the Missouri to trade. This blocking of the trail from the west by the Tetons was aimed less at hampering the Kiowas than it was designed to hurt the Arickaras. The Teton mounted warriors had no hope of storming the fortified villages of the Arickaras by direct assault but they could cut off both the trading parties from the west and the hunters who wanted to go to the buffalo herds. To further their plans for harming the Arickaras the Tetons spent a large part of each summer out about fifty miles west of the Missouri where they could produce the greatest disturbance.

In the face of this steady Teton harassment the Kiowas gave up any attempts to visit the Arickaras and turned to the Mandan villages farther up the Missouri to the north for their trade goods. This trade with the Mandans continued for several years, at least until 1803. Two years later the Indians from several of the small tribes, including the Kiowas, Kiowa Apaches, and Gataka Apaches, assembled in a large camp near the north slope of the Black Hills to prepare for a trading visit to the Mandans. With their total combined forces of more than three hundred warriors they could beat off any probable Teton attack, but for some reason they never did reach the Mandan villages. It is possible that they did not even start. While there is no report of any heavy fighting in that area in the summer of 1805, it is possible that the scouts brought word that a very large war party of Tetons was on the prowl.

Following the collapse of their plans most of the people in the camp moved off to the south in a group that included all the Kiowas, Kiowa Apaches, and Gataka Apaches, three thousand or more people in all. They crossed the Platte Valley and joined the main body of Kiowas in western Kansas. There is no further mention of the Gataka Apaches as a separate group after this trek. They either amalgamated with the Kiowa Apaches or drifted away in small groups to join their kinsmen in southeastern Arizona. Seemingly the northern Comanches accepted all of these newcomers from the north as part of the Kiowa group and so as allies from the start. There is no hint that this migration caused any friction in their new home.

In their twenty years of separation the two divisions of the Kiowas had carried on extensive programs in two different sections of the country, with only casual communications between the two. They did not work together on anything during this time, nor did they even approach within a couple of hundred miles of each other.

While the northern band of Kiowas was the smaller, and had remained in one place, it was mentioned more often by the fur traders, for it was within the area served by the Missouri posts and some of the band visited one or another of the posts almost every year. Although the southern band was much more powerful and was much more active, it received much less mention, for it never visited any trading posts but kept well out in the Plains. Any attempt to depict the activities of these two groups for the period 1785–1805 as those of a unified tribe will produce distorted accounts, while treating the two separately can produce a logical pattern of action containing few discrepancies.

While the Kiowas were undergoing these several adjustments, the Cheyennes were also forced to seek new lands and new ways of living. When they moved from the Lake Traverse area on the Minnesota-Dakota border they continued as farming people, choosing a site to the northwest on the Sheyenne River that flows down from Devil's Lake and makes a great sweep to the south before swinging off to the northeast to join the Red River. On this southern bend, on a bluff overlooking the river, the Cheyennes built a strongly fortified town, guarded by a deep ditch and a palisaded wall. The bluff was adjacent to a wide expanse of fertile land suitable for crops.

In a few years this new settlement had developed into a prosperous farming center with a well-fed, growing population. Under careful management and with some animals secured by raiding parties working far away to the southwest, the horse herd was built up until it furnished an adequate number of good mounts for all the hunters. They were quite successful in their hunting and could usually find a herd of buffalo within fifty miles or so of the town at almost any time of the year.

But this happy state was too good to last. About 1790 these farmers suffered a new disaster that crept up on them from the northeast. There in the open forests the Ojibways gathered with plans to wipe out the Cheyenne settlements and so gain control of all the surrounding country. They had just secured an ample supply of new guns from the British traders around Lake Superior and were anxious to use them on any enemies within reach. In later years they justified their sneak attack on the Cheyennes by claiming the Cheyennes had really started the war. According to the Ojibways, they had been doing some trading with the Cheyennes when one day they discovered that a Cheyenne hunter visiting them was carrying a fresh Ojibway scalp. From this they concluded that the Cheyennes should be blamed for all the Ojibways who had been lost over the past several months and so the entire town was to be destroyed to satisfy the blood debt that was owing for these many killings.

This Ojibway story appeared many years after the fighting and was probably invented to cover up their unprovoked attack on their neighbors. Just before the fighting started the Ojibways had discussed plans for doing away with the Cheyenne town, then moving to the south to turn their guns on the Dakotas and drive them from some of their rice swamps.

For a time the Ojibways were rather dubious about attacking such a stronghold as the Cheyenne settlement. They had no hope of storming the defenses so they planned a rather clever bit of trickery to gain an easy entrance. By doing some careful scouting in advance they learned that the Cheyenne hunters followed a regular routine when they went out after buffalo. They caught up their horses in the early morning and rode off in a body toward the southwest where they soon disappeared from sight behind the first ridge. When a large party went hunting it was usually away for one or two nights.

The Ojibways organized a large war party and camped in the trees well to the northeast of the town. Then when the scouts saw the Cheyennes bringing in their horses and saddling up for a hunt, they hurried to bring up the warriors. As soon as the hunters were well on their way, the Ojibways slipped through the undefended gates and killed everyone they could find, but they learned later that three or four old women had hidden themselves so well they escaped. The victors then set fire to all the lodges and scurried to safety in the forest. They dared not risk a fight with the vengeful Cheyenne horsemen out in the open country.

The Cheyenne hunters learned of the attack, probably by seeing the columns of smoke rising from their burning homes and came dashing back too late to strike even one blow against the fleeing enemy. All they found were the ashes of their homes, the mangled bodies of their families, and the old women who had a sorry tale to tell.

The disheartened men, bereft of their women and children, abandoned their farms and crops and went off across the Plains to the southwest, far from the woods and their hateful enemies. They finally reached the Missouri River where they joined the other Cheyennes who had gone directly across from Lake Traverse some ten years earlier. They started life anew, building small villages with large earth lodges and laying out some small farms, but they relied more and more on the buffalo herds to supply their food needs. While this influx of a large body of fighting men greatly increased the strength of the Cheyennes, several years elapsed before they recovered fully from the loss of so many women and children.

The next chapter in Cheyenne history is a little confused, for in later years both the Cheyennes and the Tetons claimed that the two tribes had never fought each other, but there is a rather clear record from the early traders up the Missouri that there was a period of hostilities lasting about fifteen years, the fighting consisting almost entirely of small raids by mounted bands of Tetons from the east. They stole the ripening corn and trampled the gardens, seemingly only because the Cheyenne villages were at hand, not because these villagers were considered enemies. Their primary objective was to harass the Arickaras on up the river, so they crossed the Missouri just above the Cheyenne villages and raided to the north. They also hunted west toward the Black Hills. After about fifteen years of this harassment from the various Dakota bands the Cheyennes gave up farming entirely and moved on west to become nomadic hunters. The Sutaios at this time became an integral part of the tribe.

The westward push of the Cheyennes came the same summer that the Kiowas and their allies left the Black Hills region to go south to Kansas. It is not clear whether the Cheyennes exerted any pressure on these people and so hastened their departure, or whether these Indians moved out first and the Cheyennes merely moved into the vacant space. At any rate they occupied some of the land formerly held by the Gataka Apaches, but for the most part they stayed just to the east of the Black Hills for several years.

A few of the older Cheyenne women still planted small corn patches near the sites of their winter camps as late as 1840, even though the Cheyennes had turned to the buffalo for their needs more than thirty years earlier. They became excellent hunters and fine mounted warriors almost overnight. White men who met them a few years later had no idea that these dashing horsemen had ever been farmers.

Oglalas and Tetons

In 1780 the Dakota tribe was by far the largest of all the Plains tribes with an estimated population of 25,000, about as large as the next two combined, the Blackfeet with 15,000 and the Comanches with 12,000. These three tribes together contained about one-half of all the Plains Indians and were growing steadily. It is understandable that their quest for living room for their increasing numbers should dominate the Plains history for the next fifty-seven years, the period between the two large smallpox epidemics.

While the smallpox in 1781 ravaged some of the Dakota bands, there are no firsthand estimates of the losses incurred. The nomadic bands of the Dakotas ranged far across the Plains well beyond any of the fur posts. While presumably they suffered heavier losses than the Santee bands still living in their villages in Minnesota, for the nomads were in contact with the tribes along the Missouri that had the pox, the traders reached only the Santee villages and so reported only on them.

In the absence of any reports of losses among the Santees, it would seem that the Dakotas could not have lost more than a few thousand people in all their bands, and by 1782 might have totaled nearly a third of all the Plains Indians. Their great numbers enabled them to fan out into the buffalo country and dispossess many of the smaller tribes. Their expansion to the west proceeded with no serious check until 1850.

The Dakotas were divided into several large groups, each of which might have been considered an individual tribe. The largest group was called the Santees and numbered about twelve thousand in 1782, well over half the entire tribe. At that time they still lived in their old home villages in the Minnesota lake region, where the bulk of them remained until they were finally forced out by the soldiers in 1862. It is well to keep this fact in mind when the activities of the nomadic bands are considered, or one might be strongly inclined to visualize the whole Dakota nation moving through the buffalo country in overwhelming numbers.

Most of the nomadic bands in 1782 were included in the Oglala, Teton, or Brulé groups, with as many as four thousand people in each of the first two, and with the maximum number of fighting men in each group about seven hundred to eight hundred. When the Oglalas and Tetons moved out to contest with other tribes for new hunting grounds, they were not able to advance in overwhelming numbers. Not until after 1860 were the Dakotas able to muster two or three thousand warriors in the field in a body, and then for a very short time only.

While the westward movement of the small Dakota bands had begun early in the eighteenth century, it did not cause much dislocation of any other tribes until after 1781, for these bands were occupying open grasslands between the western border of Minnesota and the Missouri River, lands which at that time were still empty of other hunters. The Oglalas and Tetons were able to scatter over this whole area gaining their entire living from the buffalo. From 1781 on they had enough horses to equip all their hunters, but it was well into the nineteenth century before they had an adequate number of pack animals. Although the Dakotas secured a large number of animals each year from the southwest, most of them through raids on the herds of other tribes, it took many years to build up enough mounts and pack animals for all the ten thousand people in the many small bands.

From about 1760 on the Oglalas, Tetons, and Brulés were able to kill all the buffalo they needed for meat and robes, although they sometimes suffered for a short period when the herds changed their feeding grounds. But these nomads felt poor, for they were very short on trade goods, especially guns, knives, cloth, blankets, needles, pots and pans, and beauty aids. Their open Plains contained few fur-bearing animals of the species whose pelts were sought by the traders. While a trader could use a few robes and a good supply of pemmican each year, he needed many packs of fine furs to take back to the eastern markets to pay off his debts and restock his packs for the next year. While the tanned buffalo robes were of real value for keeping people warm in the winter, they were too bulky and heavy to be transported at a profit from the Plains to the distant market. Not until the arrival of the river steamboats did such robes loom large in the yearly reports of the trading posts around the Plains.

Understandably all the buffalo robes, pemmican, and fresh meat the traders could use bought only a small fraction of the trade goods greatly desired by ten thousand nomads. Although these people were numerous, their entire yearly trade was so insignificant that seldom could a trader afford to even visit the hunting bands. Instead they remained at their fur posts, built near the Santee villages where they could be serviced by fleets of canoes and boats, and where the surrounding country provided the pelts of greater value per pound.

Fortunately for the buffalo hunters, they had been accustomed for many years to trade dried meat and robes to the Santees for wild rice. The Santees could use a great deal more of the buffalo products than their wild rice could buy, so they secured the rest by offering the trade goods they had bought with their furs. Acting thus as middlemen between the nomads and the traders, they enjoyed a profitable trade for many years.

Over on the Missouri, on the western edge of the nomads' hunting grounds, the village-dwelling Arickaras built up a similar profitable trade with the western Oglala and Teton bands. The Arickaras lived in strongly fortified villages, safe from any assault by the nomads. They were visited each year by French traders who came up the river from St. Louis in boats with their goods. Although there was some bickering and fighting at times between the Arickaras and the Tetons, most of the time until about 1790 both groups found it to their mutual advantage to maintain peaceful relations. Also this opportunity to trade each year on the Missouri gave the nomads a larger market for their meat and robes, and led them to spend more time along the western edge of their hunting grounds, leaving the eastern portion of the grasslands less crowded and thus available for the new Dakota bands pushed out of the lake country. Although this trade was profitable for the Arickaras, it was too small to tempt the French to build a post near the villages. Not until after the weakened Arickaras moved on up the Missouri in the 1820s did the fur men decide to build posts to trade directly with the Tetons and Oglalas along the Missouri near the sites of the nomads' winter camps.

As early as 1775 small raiding parties of Dakotas scouted the country across the Missouri toward the Black Hills. That summer a noted warrior, Standing Bull,[1] went far beyond any previous venture and was amazed to see the dark mass of the Black Hills in the distance looming far above the horizon. In all his life he had never seen any elevations higher than the hills and bluffs along the Missouri and these forest-clad mountains impressed him mightily. This far venture of Standing Bull is of special interest for it shows plainly that none of the Dakota war parties had ever gone that far west of the Missouri before 1775. The smallpox six years later and the necessary adjustments following that disaster kept the Dakota bands confined to the lands east of the Missouri until about 1790.

After the Cheyennes gathered along the Missouri about 1790 they suffered Dakota raids each year as the traditions of both tribes state. Writers who wrongly assume that the Cheyennes had moved on west to the Black Hills at a much earlier date cite these raids as proving the presence of Teton bands in the Black Hills in the eighteenth century, but since the Cheyennes did not leave their villages on the banks of the Missouri until 1803–07, raids against them any earlier did not put the raiders west of the river.

As more and more of the Dakotas left the Minnesota lake country and became nomadic hunters, their raids to the west increased in size and violence. After 1790 many fairly large war parties crossed the Missouri and ranged along the west bank, never going very far west of the river. In 1795 a large war party of Dakotas blocked the trail from the Kiowa camps on the Little Missouri to the Arickara villages as was mentioned previously. This blockade was only a few miles to the west of the Missouri and marked the western limit of the Dakota intrusion that year. While some of the war parties took some women along to do camp chores, there is no indication that any of the bands moved their families across the river for year-round living until after 1800.

Even after several of the bands were living on the west bank they seldom hunted very far to the west. They do speak of being able to see the Black Hills in the distance on a clear day, but that would mean they were still fifty miles from the eastern slopes of those imposing ranges. Each year with the approach of winter these bands all withdrew to the Missouri River bottoms where they set up their winter camps. There they often were joined by other Teton and Oglala bands that still spent the entire year east of the Missouri, but during the 1820s there was a steady movement of these bands to the west. Each year a few more of them went across the river for the summer hunt and did not return to their eastern hunting grounds.

As a result of this steady migration the Dakota population west of the river increased rapidly until by 1830 about half of all the Tetons and Oglalas, and a few other scattered bands, perhaps a total of five thousand people were living permanently to the west. This whole movement was rather rapid, for the earliest account of any band actually hunting as far west as the eastern slopes of the Black Hills is dated 1805. That band did not retreat to the Missouri when winter came, but pitched their winter camp near Bear Butte.

Blackfoot Aggression

The Blackfeet, like the other Plains tribes, were estimated to have lost at least one third of their people to the smallpox in 1781, and entered the new period with a total population of about seven thousand, divided rather evenly into three large bands that some authorities feel should really be considered as separate tribes. These were the Northern Blackfeet, living in central Alberta, the Bloods, to the west along the foothills of the Rockies and as far south as the Montana border, and the Piegans, who moved south of the Bow River as soon as the smallpox had wiped out the Shoshoni band there.

The Northern Blackfeet were friendly neighbors of the small Athapascan tribe, the Sarsis, and the Assiniboins on down the Saskatchewan Valley to the southeast. For many years the Blackfeet and the Assiniboins had been friendly, even to the extent of intermarrying, but sometime about the opening of the nineteenth century the two tribes became hostile and the first forty years of the century contain many stories of conflicts between the two.

The Bloods to the west had the important task of guarding the mountain passes against any incursion of the Kutenais and any attempts of the British traders to take goods, especially guns, across the mountains to the enemies of the Blackfeet. The Piegans to the south focused most of their attention on the Marias Pass just south of Glacier Park. The Flatheads of western Montana liked to come east through this pass to hunt buffalo on the upper Marias River drainage. The Piegans also sent raiding parties far to the south into the upper Missouri drainage against the Shoshonis, and were constantly raiding the Crow country to the southeast in the Yellowstone Valley.

At the turn of the century the Blackfeet controlled a large area of excellent buffalo country, ample for a population of perhaps twenty thousand, but even when they numbered only seven thousand they felt rather confined and pushed continually to the east and south in an attempt to enlarge their holdings. According to their own accounts they were essentially a peaceful people who did not fight against anyone unless the other was the aggressor, but the fur men who traded with the tribe over a period of half a century found them, in the period 1782–1837, a very quarrelsome people, always looking for trouble. They even fought among themselves at times, with the Bloods pitted against the Piegans.

After the smallpox had spent itself, there was a short period of peace between the Piegans and the Shoshonis while these two weakened opponents reorganized and regained some of their strength. Then, according to the Piegans, the Shoshonis broke the peace in a dreadful way. Since none of the participating Shoshonis have left their version of the incident only the Piegan account can be reported here.[2]

About 1784 a Piegan hunting party of five tipis, about forty people in all, went far up the Bow River and into the mountains searching for bighorn sheep whose horns were prized, for they could be made into durable bowls and ladles. When these people did not return at the expected time, scouts searched their hunting area for their camp. They found a scene of bloody disaster, with the whole camp filled with the mutilated bodies of the missing people. Characteristic marks on sticks stuck into the ground showed that the Shoshonis had committed this deed, and had left the painted sticks to boast of their success.

A strong scouting party of about fifty men hurried off to the south, looking for the enemy, but they were much too late. After traveling south for six days, about 150 miles, they found a large Shoshoni camp well south of the Montana border, probably on a branch of the Teton River. The scouts lacked the strength to make an attack on that many of the enemy, but they lurked around for a few days, keeping well hidden and waiting for some favorable opportunity to strike a sudden blow. One evening as a storm approached they crept into the Shoshoni horse herd and each man put his lead rope on a horse or a mule. Their leader would not permit the men to try to steal any extra horses for that would disturb the herd and might lead to an attack by the Shoshonis. Instead he insisted that the safe return of all his men and with each riding a stolen horse was much better than trying to make off with the herd and losing a few scalps in the attempt. This attitude was the common one among the wise leaders of raiders throughout the Plains tribes. When the storm broke the Piegans all rode away hidden by the rain and darkness, safe from discovery.

Although the Piegans secured fifty good horses, they felt that they had not even begun to collect enough damages to pay for their lost tribesmen. In a large council meeting with leaders of all three bands, a decision was reached that they must drive out or exterminate all the Shoshonis and they began mounting systematic attacks against these enemies that eventually led the Blackfoot war parties as far south as the upper Snake Valley in southern Idaho.

Evidently the successful raid by the Piegan scouts frightened the Shoshoni camp very badly, for the next scouting party to the south found the whole country to the Missouri bare of the enemy. The Shoshonis had packed up all their gear and had left the country. A few lodges went southeast to join the Crows on the Yellowstone while the rest moved on up the Missouri beyond the Belt Mountains, then up the Jefferson Fork of the river into the Big Hole country and none of them ever tried to return to the Sun River country to hunt.

The scouting party of Piegans kept on southward up the Missouri and finally across the Continental Divide into southern Idaho. They missed the Shoshoni camps completely, for these were well to the west of the trail beyond another mountain ridge. On went the scouts into Utah, skirting the eastern shore of the Great Salt Lake and on south until they reached the Four Corners area. There they met a Spanish mule train taking a load of silver from the mines into Santa Fe. They ambushed the train, captured all the mules and horses with their gear, but the mule packs full of "white rocks" they dumped as worthless, for they had never seen silver metal. When they returned to their home camps on the Bow River their exploits were reported to David Thompson who was in the Piegan camp that summer.[3]

As soon as the Shoshonis had withdrawn from the Bow River Valley and the country just to the south the Piegans had easy access to both the Kutenais and the Flatheads who were then living part of each year in the foothills just to the east of the Rockies. This is the first time the Blackfeet had any chance to meet with these people west of the mountains, about forty or fifty years after the tribe had secured its first horses, so it is extremely doubtful that the Piegans could have secured their first animals from either of these tribes, as their traditions indicate. It is much more probable that their first horses came through sneaky raids on the Shoshoni herds many years before the Blackfeet ever met either the Flatheads or Kutenais.

One Blackfoot tradition, even more dubious, mentions the Nez Percés as the suppliers of their first horses, but the Nez Percés did not even get as far as the Flathead lands until 1780, or across the mountains into the buffalo country until after 1790. Then when they did meet the Blackfeet, it was as enemies. It is probable that the very high quality of the Nez Percé horses during the nineteenth century led both the Blackfeet and the Crows to claim that their horses came from those famous herds rather than from the despised Shoshonis.

After the Shoshonis left Sun River, the next mention of them on the upper Missouri comes from the journals of the Lewis and Clark expedition. When the party reached a spot on the Jefferson River a few miles above Three Forks in the summer of 1805, Sacajawea, a Shoshoni woman with the party, pointed out the place she had been picking berries six years earlier when she had been captured by a Hidatsa war party from North Dakota. They had come across the Montana plains between the Missouri and Yellowstone rivers, a distance of about five hundred miles, looking for Shoshoni horses to steal, and picking up a few captives such as Sacajawea in addition.

The Assiniboins and Atsinas who lived just to the north and northwest of the Hidatsas, also liked Shoshoni horses, for they too raided as far as the upper Missouri in search of them. These recurring raids from the four hostile tribes, the Blackfeet, Hidatsas, Assiniboins, and Atsinas, finally forced Sacajawea's people, the Lemhi Shoshonis, to keep to the west of the Continental Divide for safety. Only occasionally did they dare to venture into Montana to hunt buffalo and then only if they could join with a strong band of well-armed Flatheads and Nez Percés from the Columbia Basin who went regularly into the Three Forks country and on across into the Yellowstone Valley on their hunts.

No sooner had the Blackfeet rid themselves of the Shoshonis when they felt menaced from the west. David Thompson of Hudson's Bay Company built a strong new trading post west of the Continental Divide, across Crow's Nest Pass in Kutenai country. The Blackfeet were alarmed at the prospect of those redoubtable fighters, and their southern neighbors, the Montana Flatheads, securing a ready supply of guns and ammunition, thus placing themselves on a more favorable footing in their wars with the more numerous Blackfeet, the guns and the better horses of the westerners canceling the advantages of Blackfoot numbers.

The Piegan band of Blackfeet sent a large war party across Crow's Nest Pass to attack both the new post and the Kutenais who lived nearby, but the expedition had a change of mind when they saw the strength of the post and finally returned without accomplishing anything of note. The Piegans then sealed the short, easy route west by Crow's Nest Pass and forced the traders to use a route much farther north, up the Athabasca River.

Blackfeet and Americans

The first encounter between the Blackfeet and the Americans produced serious trouble between the two and convinced the Indians that the Americans should always be treated as enemies. This event occurred on the Marias River in Blackfoot territory in the summer of 1806.[4] Meriwether Lewis was on his return journey from the Pacific Coast when he took a detour to the north with three companions to get a better look at the upper course of the Marias River.

His small party traveled openly across the Plains and was not much perturbed when they met eight young Blackfeet riding up to meet them. Lewis offered the Blackfeet his friendship which they accepted. The two groups then camped together for the night. About dawn the Indians tried to steal some of the guns from the camp and one of them was stabbed to death in a scuffle for a rifle. Another Blackfoot was shot and severely wounded as he and his comrades tried to drive off the horses. After these severe losses the Indians retreated in disorder, carrying away their wounded comrade but leaving behind some of their horses and weapons.

This encounter enraged the Blackfeet who considered Lewis as the aggressor in the affair, for he had trespassed on tribal lands. To make matters worse, four white men had routed eight Blackfeet—killing one, wounding another, and then escaping unharmed with some loot. Obviously several American scalps were required to wipe out the sting of this defeat. The British traders in Alberta encouraged this enmity against the Americans and suggested that the tribe should be alert against any attempt other Americans would soon make to come up the Missouri to bring guns to Blackfoot enemies.

The British traders were quite correct in this forecast. The next year after the Lewis affair, 1807, brought trappers to the upper Missouri, working out of the new fur post on the Yellowstone at the mouth of the Big Horn River. Two of them, John Colter and John Potts, found beaver trapping excellent on the Jefferson. One summer morning about sunup, as the fog lay heavy on the water, they were taking beaver from their traps within a few hundred yards of the spot of Sacajawea's capture eight years earlier.

They heard the sound of many horses approaching, but before they could drift out of danger the fog suddenly lifted and they found themselves within a few feet of two hundred mounted Blackfoot warriors on the river bank. Instead of surrendering quietly to the Blackfoot demand, Potts grabbed his gun and shot into the crowd, killing one man. He died under a hail of arrows. Colter, still making no effort to resist, was taken out on the bare, wide river bottom. There he was stripped of his clothes and was forced to run across the Plain thickly studded with pricklypear clumps. The Blackfeet, looking for sport with their revenge, gave him a headstart of perhaps a hundred feet, then the whole party took after him on foot to run him down. Colter was a superb runner and stayed ahead of them for six miles until he reached the Madison River. He dove in and sought refuge in a deep eddy under a huge pile of driftwood, half-submerged in the river. The Blackfeet finally left after spending the entire day futilely searching for him. When they had gone Colter fled up the Madison in the dark, then crossed over the bare ridge to the Gallatin and on east across Bozeman Pass. He finally arrived at Fort Remon far down the Yellowstone, well tanned all over, his feet still sore from the pricklypear spines, but otherwise in good health. He had fed adequately if not sumptuously on ripe berries and young, fat gophers along the way.

Three years later, in 1810, the Missouri Fur Company under Manuel Lisa sent a large party of trappers to build a strong post at the Three Forks so they could trap the rich beaver country. They soon finished their post but they did little trapping. They found themselves under constant attacks from the Blackfeet who lurked in the surrounding hills all summer. After losing most of their horses, and having twenty of their men killed, they abandoned the post and moved out, some of them going back to the Yellowstone, the rest up the Madison and across into southern Idaho. That summer the Piegans had been very busy with David Thompson's new post among the Kutenais and had left the fighting at Three Forks to the Bloods who had some help from the Atsinas.

Another of the Piegan problems that year was caused by a large party of Flatheads. They had a new supply of guns from a new post near their country and decided to risk going across the Rockies to their old hunting grounds just to the east of Marias Pass. There they were attacked by a large Piegan war party that they beat back after a hard fight, killing sixteen of the enemy. To the Piegans this was a grievous loss and made them much more cautious in attacking Flatheads in the future. They also were more firmly convinced than ever that they should use every means at their command to bar all American fur men from Montana and thus cut down the flow of guns to the Flatheads. But the new trading posts in the Columbia Basin built during the period 1809–14, insured a steady supply of guns and ammunition to the Flatheads and to their allies, the Nez Perces, a supply that the Blackfeet could not interrupt. Both of these western tribes had a surplus of good horses that the fur men needed and so could afford good guns.

For years the Flatheads and Nez Percés had hunted buffalo west of the Continental Divide, in the Bitterroot and Deer Lodge valleys. Now they extended their activities across the Divide to the east, into the upper Missouri drainage, and on across Bozeman Pass into the Yellowstone Valley. They then spread out to the north to the wide plains just east of the Crazy Mountains and still well to the south of Blackfoot country.

Each year the Columbia Basin people met in large camps in August to harvest the camas bulbs and the huckleberries on the plateau. There people from many villages and several tribes met and there some of them would make up one or more large hunting parties to go across the mountains where they might stay until the next summer or even for five more summers before they came home. These parties were always well organized and each one was led by one or more experienced warriors, with a head chief elected for the trip. They were all rugged fighters, well armed and well mounted, and effectually prevented the Blackfeet from expanding to the west of Sun River or into the upper Missouri country, although large Blackfoot war parties, and at times Blackfoot hunting parties, stayed on the upper Missouri for months at a time.

Not satisfied with fighting against the Kutenais, Shoshonis, Flatheads, and Nez Percés, the Blackfeet also sent their war parties each year to attack the Crows on the Yellowstone. Although these two tribes were separated by two hundred miles of open country, they carried on constant warfare. The Blackfeet tried to raid the Crow horse herds and to lift Crow scalps in their many expeditions in force as far as the Yellowstone River, some of them even in the coldest spells of Montana winters. The Crows in turn raided Blackfoot camps in the Judith Basin of central Montana and along Sun River west of Great Falls.

The Blackfeet had a formal method of organizing large war parties something on the same pattern as used by the Iroquois. At a large encampment in early summer they chose a body of men, estimated by the fur men at eight hundred to nine hundred, who went out in two, three, or four groups to attack foes at a distance. By attacking each of their important foes at least once each summer they were able to hold all the land they had seized by 1812, but they were never able to extend their holdings any farther in any direction.

Since the Blackfeet had increased steadily in numbers from 1781 on, they had a population of several thousand by 1812 with perhaps 1,800 warriors. By using about half of these each summer for offensive operations, they still were able to maintain strong guards for their own camps. Their organized and disciplined war parties numbered from two hundred to six hundred men, according to the mountain men who encountered them in Montana and fought with them each summer. The Blackfeet marched in a solid body when near their enemies, traveling on foot until they turned homeward when all who had been able to steal horses along the way could ride back in comfort.

Even with these formidable forces in the field the Blackfeet came under increasing pressure from both the mountain men and the combined Flathead-Nez Percé forces, who came boldly across the mountain passes to challenge the Blackfeet on the hunting grounds.

During the same period mountain men from two or three American companies and from the Hudson's Bay Company trapped in south-western Montana, and that beautiful, mountain girt land, well stocked with game, fur-bearing animals, and fish, became the scene of most of the fighting between red men and white, although at times the conflict spread across into southern Idaho.

Blackfoot resentment and enmity against the Flatheads grew year by year as their losses mounted under the fire of the new guns. In time they elevated the Flatheads to the rank of their most hated foe, especially as the weakened Shoshonis fled farther to the south. And they hated the mountain men who trapped the mountain streams the Blackfeet claimed as their own, taking Blackfoot beaver, eating Blackfoot buffalo, and at times lifting Blackfoot scalps.

In their winter councils they finally decided that in 1832 they would go south with more warriors than usual and wipe out both the Flatheads and the mountain men in one sustained campaign if it took all year to do it. From early spring until the winter snows blew in, the war parties raged throughout the whole land with the fighting and raiding scattered far and wide wherever an enemy could be found. Time and again they attacked camps, small trapping parties, isolated travelers, and always the enemy horse herds. On the whole they met with indifferent success, their gains wiped out by their losses. While they killed many of their enemies and collected quantities of loot and herds of horses, their own losses in warriors were heavy. At the end of the fighting they withdrew without having accomplished either of their aims for both the Flatheads and the mountain men continued to dispute the territory with them. So this indecisive warfare raged on but on a smaller scale for five more years.

Meanwhile the Blackfeet were adjusting to a new situation in central Montana. There on the Missouri River well below the Great Falls of the Missouri, the American Fur Company had succeeded in building a post in 1831, Fort Piegan. It was replaced the following year by Fort McKenzie. With this new post the Company succeeded in diverting much of the trade of the Blackfeet to the Americans, an astonishing feat when it is remembered that the Blackfeet had been bitter enemies of all Americans since 1806. The post was run by Alexander Culbertson who was married to a girl from the Blood band and was well liked by the tribe. He secured the goodwill of the Blackfeet by promising to keep all his men away from their streams. They should trap their own furs and bring them to the post where he would pay them top prices.

By encouraging a more systematic trapping of the beaver, Culbertson built up his trade. He also was able to buy tanned buffalo robes at a good price, taking all that were offered, for with his boats he could carry the heavy robes down the river to St. Louis at a profit while the British traders in Alberta could not afford to buy items of such little value per pound when they had to transport them overland to market.

From Fort McKenzie have come several eye-witness accounts exemplifying the quarrelsome nature of all the Blackfeet, especially the Bloods. When a trader at the fort gave an especially elaborate military outfit to Bull's Tail of the Blackfeet, the Bloods decided that their own leader had been insulted because his gift was less elaborate. In their eyes their leader, Thunder in the Hills, was the more important of the two. They killed Bull's Tail's nephew to emphasize their point and so brought new bloodshed within the tribe.

The Blackfeet really had plenty of enemies without indulging in such fighting within their own ranks. Both the Assiniboins and Crees had a large number of scores against them for past attacks. A large force of these two combined in a surprise attack against a small Piegan camp near the fort and killed forty of their foes with the loss of only six of their own men. Then Blackfoot reinforcements came dashing in from a large camp a few miles away, but they arrived with their horses so badly winded that they could not catch the Assiniboins and Crees. The two forces then moved warily about, keeping at a safe distance from each other all day, for there was too much risk in a general melee for either to attack.

The whole incident has been well publicized by an artist, Charles Bodmer, who was on hand to get the scenes necessary to illustrate the details of the first bloody attack, and with him were several whites who wrote or told their own versions later. It is obvious that many more such encounters took place in the open Plains when there were no literate observers to jot down the details.

Thus the Blackfeet carried on, ranging far and wide across Montana, fighting almost everybody in sight, until finally a new plague dampened their spirits.

Oglalas and Cheyennes

Year by year the Dakota raids to the west increased in size and violence, but they met with strong resistance from several of the tribes living along the Missouri. The Omahas and Poncas, living in the same area along the west bank of the Missouri River near the Nebraska-South Dakota line, were well supplied with both horses and guns—the horses from the Pawnees and the guns from the French traders who came to their villages each year. For a time they acted as middlemen, selling off some of their trade goods to the Oglala bands hunting to the northeast of their land, but about 1789 the Oglalas became troublesome and serious fighting broke out with strong war parties from each side moving out to make attacks on the enemies. All of this fighting was carried out east of the Missouri and lasted for three years until the two groups met and concluded a peace agreement in the winter of 1791–92.

Part of the Omaha success in this war occurred because the Oglalas and their allies, the Brulés, were busy at the time with other attacks against the Cheyenne villages on the Missouri, well to the north of the Omahas. The Cheyenne farmers in their fortified villages held off the Dakota raiders until 1803, blocking their way to the west. The Dakotas could send war parties across the river, but if they kept well to the north of those people they were in danger from the Arickaras. Such was the situation when the Dakota war party blocked the trail from the Kiowa villages on the Little Missouri to the Arickaras. If the locations of the villages of the Omahas, Cheyennes, and Arickaras are plotted on a map, then the pattern of fighting for this period, 1790–1803, is easy to grasp. It is evident at a glance that all of the fighting between the Missouri River tribes and the Oglalas took place close to the river, some of it along the east bank, the rest out on the Plains to the northeast.

The Dakotas reported that they had their first clashes with the Crows during this same period. At that time the Crows had reached their permanent homeland on the Yellowstone River from Powder River west to the Big Horn. The Crows had always had friendly relations with the Mandans ever since the Hidatsa-Crow people moved southwest from Devil's Lake to the Missouri, and this relationship continued after the Crows split away from the Hidatsas and moved on up the Missouri. They had been accustomed to send a few men to the Mandan villages for trade goods ever since the Verendryes had brought the first French goods from the Red River Valley to the Mandans in 1729, when the Crows were about at the mouth of the Yellowstone. This Crow-Mandan trade continued until the traders from St. Louis built a fur post at the mouth of the Big Horn River in 1807.

From the Dakota accounts and from the positions occupied by the various tribes, especially the Kiowas and the Kiowa Apaches from 1785 to 1805, it is obvious that the only feasible location for any hostile meeting between the Crow trading parties and the wide-ranging Dakota raiders was along this trail to the Mandan villages and within fifty miles or less of the Mandans. These affairs involved only a few men on each side and resulted in very small losses. Dakota raids on the main Crow horse herds and camps along the Powder River had to wait until after the departure of the Kiowas and Kiowa Apaches about 1805 had left the Little Missouri area vacant and so permitted the Dakotas to occupy the grounds west of the Missouri to the Black Hills and along their northern slopes.

Once the Cheyennes had established themselves as nomadic hunters around the southern end of the Black Hills, they became much more prosperous and enjoyed more peace than they had known as farmers for many years. As nomads they were less exposed to raids, and they no longer raised corn and other crops that the raiders wanted. Also they soon became formidable fighters on horseback, able to hold their own against the Oglalas, for at that time the two were about equal in strength. Once the Oglalas found that there was no profit for them in fighting the Cheyennes they became much less hostile and soon set up regular trading meetings with their former enemies. By 1830 the Cheyenne trade attracted the regular fur men and a small post was built especially to deal with the Cheyennes. It was located on the Cheyenne River just below the forks.

Then two men who had been busy trading between St. Louis and New Mexico, William and Charles Bent,[5] changed the entire growth pattern of the western Plains and brought about a major redistribution of the tribes by building a large, strong post of adobe bricks on the north bank of the Arkansas River. On their way east from a trading trip to Taos they were traveling down the Arkansas to the mouth of Purgatory Creek. There they paused and made camp inside a small temporary stockade, for they were in an area crisscrossed by many hostile Indian bands. They were soon visited by a war party that came charging up from the south driving a large horse herd.

These visitors were Cheyennes on their way home after a successful raid on the Comanches. They were deeply interested in Bent's proposal for a permanent fur post on the Arkansas and promised to trade with him as soon as his post was built.

So the great post, famous throughout the Plains as Bent's Fort, was built over a period of two years, and was opened for trade in 1833 even before the construction was completed. That summer about half of the Cheyenne tribe drifted south from their Black Hills location. About three hundred fifty lodges took up their hunting grounds in the vicinity of the post, working to the north and northeast. They became known as the Southern Cheyennes and lived along the Kansas-Colorado border for the next thirty years.

To counter the competition offered by Bent's Fort and to hold some of the trade of the western nomadic bands, William Sublette and Robert Campbell built a small post on the Laramie fork of the North Platte a short distance from its mouth. This post soon grew into a large log fort, usually called Fort Laramie, and was opened for business in 1834.

Other fur traders had already built a number of small posts and forts west of the Missouri near the Black Hills, one on White River near Pine Ridge, one on Cheyenne River at the mouth of Cherry Creek, and another at the forks of the Cheyenne. In spite of all these new posts, Campbell was able to persuade about half of the Oglalas, one hundred lodges, to leave their hunting grounds east of the Black Hills, where they had been for about thirty years, and move out west to Fort Laramie. This group was followed the next spring by the remainder of the Oglalas and the combined group was strong enough to take over the old Cheyenne and Arapaho hunting grounds between the forks of the Platte. The Cheyennes offered little opposition to this move, for they were well established off to the south near Bent's Fort, and they considered the buffalo hunting in western Kansas superior to that around Fort Laramie. Before any more large tribal adjustments could be made, the northern Plains were visited by another smallpox epidemic.

12

The Great Scourge Returns

IN 1836 NOMADIC BANDS OF BUFFALO HUNTERS were scattered all over the northern Plains and had reached a rather satisfactory level of living. The horse herds had been built up to adequate size, although there never was a band of Indians on the Plains that would admit to having enough horses. The people were well clothed and well fed, and even the dogs were eating well, for the hunters were killing more buffalo than their camps could use. They needed extra hides from the cows for their women to tan into robes for the coming summer trade.

Through the fall and winter the women labored from dawn till dusk. They never had enough time to care for all the meat from the kills, and the piles of untanned hides by the tipis grew and grew although the women worked steadily on their tanning chores every spare moment.

This great new demand for robes had come with the arrival of the first steamboat up the Missouri in 1832,[1] bringing up the trade goods and taking downriver all the robes the tribes could supply—robes that had been too bulky and heavy to attract the traders until this new means of transportation was developed. Hence the excessive killing of cow buffaloes in the fall hunts, bringing the wastage of meat and the extra work for the women.

So all the northern tribes and upriver trading posts were looking forward to a great trading season when the steamer *St. Peter's* should arrive with the bales and boxes of all sorts of trade goods. In June 1837, the *St. Peter's* came surging up against the spring current, high with melting snows and dotted with drifting timber. At each fur post along the way Indian bands were waiting impatiently with their piles of robes to trade for guns, ammunition, knives, pots, cloth, blankets, beads, and trinkets, with some firewater, too.

But not all the *St. Peter's* cargo was desirable, for lurking aboard were the deadly smallpox germs. Unknown even to Captain Bernard Pratte, one of his men on board carried the smallpox infection. By the time the steamer had unloaded its cargo at Fort Clark, four of the people aboard had broken out with the disease. Trader Francis Chardon tried to keep the Indians away from the boat, but he found that an impossible task. They would not believe that they, too, might catch the pox, even after they had been warned repeatedly of the danger.

Soon the exposed Indians had reached the highly infectious stage and were running high fevers, but by the time they realized that they were sick indeed, it was too late. All their families and friends had been exposed to the pox and had spread it to other bands and villages. So the pox swept through the Mandan villages like a prairie fire, leaving the dead strewn all around, for there were not enough healthy people left even to drag the bodies from the lodges. By autumn when the pox had run its course only a hundred Mandans were alive of a tribe of 1,600 in the village in June.

The daily report written at Fort Clark by the trader Chardon gives in detail the trials of the Mandans. Although there was no observer at hand to witness and record the epidemic among the nomadic bands in the vicinity, it is certain that the pattern was much the same once the infection reached a camp. Quite often it was picked up from one band by an enemy and carried home to his own people. In such fashion the Dakota raiders who took advantage of the helpless condition of the fever-stricken Mandans to raid their horse herds and corn fields while the dying victims could do nothing to stop them, picked up the smallpox as a part of their loot and carried it back to their bands. Soon they had passed it along to other bands as far south as Fort Pierre.

The Hidatsas and Arickaras had been away from the river on their summer hunts when the smallpox arrived and they were cautioned to stay out on the Plains until fall, but they wanted to harvest their corn.

They returned to their villages too soon, harvested the crops, caught the pox, and suffered heavy losses, but lighter than the Mandans. While their villages survived, they were very weak after 1837.

When the Pawnees in Nebraska learned that their Oglala neighbors were in serious trouble in their camps in southern South Dakota, they sent out war parties against the invalids. Their easy initial success in their attack spelled their doom, for the pox went home with them in the Oglala scalps. The disease finally died out that fall in the Pawnee villages and so the tribes to the south escaped.

On up the Missouri at Fort Union the tragedy at Fort Clark was repeated with a few added details. When the people in the fort fell ill, Jacob Halsey, the trader in charge, attempted to keep the Assiniboins away from the fort until the disease had passed, but they were anxious to trade and pitched their camp close by. One night two of their young men scaled the pickets of the horse corral and stole two of the best horses. Four employees from the fort chased and caught them, and persuaded them to give back the animals, but in the prolonged negotiations the Assiniboins caught the pox from one of the men. They in turn spread it among their people and a large number, about half the entire tribe, died before winter.

Another employee inadvertently took the pox with him up the Yellowstone when he went with the year's supply of goods for Fort Cass in the Crow country. The Crows still retained a strong tribal tradition of the horrors of the epidemic of 1781 and moved far away from the fort until winter, hiding in the Wyoming mountains. The Wind River Shoshonis were just as prudent, so these two tribes suffered no deaths from the pox that year.

A keelboat from Fort Union moved on up the Missouri bound for Fort McKenzie at the head of navigation on the river. By this time Fort McKenzie was handling all the trade of the Blackfeet on the American side of the border, and had an encampment of 500 lodges of Piegans and Bloods waiting for the trade goods to arrive so they could turn in their many thousand buffalo robes for their needed supplies.

Although all of the keelboat crew seemed to be healthy when they left Fort Union, two of them became feverish about the time they reached the mouth of the Judith River a hundred or so miles downriver from their destination. The boat captain, Alexander Harvey, then tied up his boat and sent word on to Fort McKenzie of his plight.

Albert Culbertson, who was then in command of the post, told the assembled Blackfeet of the sickness on the boat and that it must wait downstream until the people recovered so they would not give the disease to the Indians, but they would not believe him. They feared that this was just another white man's trick to cheat them. They declared that if he did not order the boat to come on at once, they would ride down and get it. Since any such action on the part of the Blackfeet would give them all the pox, and would probably result in the loss of most of the cargo to the detriment of the company's profits, Culbertson ordered Harvey to proceed.

After the boat arrived at the post two of the crew died of the pox, but the Blackfeet still were not convinced that they were in any danger. While Culbertson did his best to keep the Blackfeet from any direct contact with the sick, the five thousand Blackfeet swarmed into the post and in five hectic days of trading had secured all their goods, including large supplies of guns and ammunition. This they wanted very badly for their forthcoming attacks on their various enemies, particularly the Crows and Flatheads. Then they broke camp and hastened away from the contagion, going off to the northwest across the open Plains. Shortly after the Blackfeet had left the entire garrison of the post caught the pox. One of the men and twenty-six of the Indian wives of the engages died. During this time of travail the post was left in peace. Not even one Indian showed up for further trade that summer.

Finally Culbertson decided that something must be wrong. He set out with a small party to follow the Blackfoot trail toward their homeland. Only a few days along the trail, at the forks of the Marias, he found the Blackfoot camp, a camp of the dead. Only two old women who as girls had survived the epidemic of 1781 still lived. In spite of the precautions of both the traders and the Indians, the infection had made its way from the fort to the Indian camp and had finished its incubation period after the band had been on the homeward trail a few days. The Blackfoot tribe as a whole lost more than one-half its total population with the Piegans and Bloods suffering more severely than the Northern Blackfeet who had not gone to Fort McKenzie.

Thus in a single summer the Blackfeet were reduced from a dominant position on the northern Plains to a badly shaken band of impotent survivors, for the shock of their losses numbed the fighting spirit of the survivors. After 1837 the Blackfeet were too weak and disorganized to wage any offensive war for several years. Even after they had recovered from their losses, their sadness and sense of guilt over their misfortunes kept them brooding for a long time. Blackfoot aggression against other tribes had ended. No longer did they seek to expand their holdings, but even gave up some of the land they had held for several years.

Word of the Blackfoot disaster soon reached the tribes across the mountains to the west. The Flatheads and Nez Percés, together with reinforcements from other Columbia Basin tribes, came boldly through the Rocky Mountain passes to hunt where they wished, feeling themselves strong enough to ward off any possible Blackfoot attack. They even dared to camp and hunt along Sun River, and with their friends, the Crows, dominated the fine grasslands of the Judith Basin. So matters stood in central Montana until government officials came through in 1855 and induced the several tribes to sign peace treaties with one another.

Although the smallpox scourge brought nothing but disaster to most of the tribes on the northern Plains, for the Dakotas their gains offset their losses. The Pawnees in Nebraska were so weakened by their heavy losses to the plague that they caught from the Oglala scalps that they were no longer a threat to the Oglalas in their new hunting grounds on the North Platte River. Even the Pawnee raids on other Dakota bands near the Missouri dwindled until they caused very little trouble.

More important to the Teton bands of the Dakotas was the virtual elimination of the Arickaras and Mandans along the Missouri. For nearly a century the fortified villages of these two tribes had successfully resisted all Dakota attacks, and had blocked any attempts by those people to cross the Missouri within miles of their villages. Now the Mandans had ceased to exist as a tribe. The few survivors went upriver and became a part of the Hidatsas. The Arickaras were still able to maintain a small village, but they were no threat to anyone. Now that these two tribes, the Mandans and the Arickaras, no longer offered any opposition to Teton movements, that tribe could cross the Missouri wherever they liked.

That the new freedom of movement was important to the Tetons is shown by their actions. In the spring of 1838, only a few months after the plague, Teton bands were moving from the James River country across the Missouri to take over permanently all of western North Dakota south of the Missouri. This included the entire basin of the

Little Missouri and brought them to the border of the Powder River country. There they were halted by the Crows who held them to the Little Missouri drainage for another twenty years.

During this period after the epidemic, from 1837 to 1851 (when the great council meeting was called at Fort Laramie), less than two-fifths of all the Dakota people lived west of the Missouri. The larger portion of the tribe was scattered across the Plains in eastern North and South Dakota, or were still in their Minnesota villages, most of them among the lakes and rice swamps. Few people realize how tardy the Dakotas were in leaving their homes in the woodland fringe and their hunting grounds in the eastern part of the Dakotas.

This lag in the westward movement of the Dakotas explains in a large part the ability of the Crows to hold back the Teton bands for a long period. When the Tetons went on west in 1838 they had about five thousand people in all their bands, not too many more than the Crows who are usually estimated at four thousand during this period. Since the Tetons had no sort of organization that would enable them to bring all their strength against the Crows, they were successful against those excellent warriors only when they could stage surprise attacks on small hunting bands in the Powder River country.

At times war parties of young men from the several hunting bands of Dakotas still living east of the Missouri went west during the summer in search of adventure and danger. They would join up with the Tetons for a few days for some large action, but they usually went home during the fall. The large Santee group that lived in Minnesota, usually considered to be from one-half to three-fifths of all the Dakotas, seemingly were never seriously involved in any of the expansion to the west of the Missouri before 1862.

The combination of these two groups of Dakotas, the one sedentary and clinging to its village homes, the other nomadic and spreading far and wide through the buffalo country, gave the Dakotas by far the largest land holdings of any Indian tribe on the Plains. The year 1850 marked the peak of this expansion. Although the nomadic Oglalas and Tetons pushed farther to the west after that year, the Santee bands began surrendering some of their holdings shortly after that time. At the peak of their power the Dakotas held an expanse of country much larger than some of the European kingdoms at the time, a country that appears at a glance to be out of all proportion to their needs. Left undisturbed by the white settlers, the Dakotas could have continued a nomadic life indefinitely on a half or a third of this acreage, needing only a little planning and forethought to make efficient use of their natural resources.

In later years, when the Dakotas looked back on the period of their greatest land holding, they indicated that all of this area really had belonged to them for a long time and they should have been allowed to continue occupying it. But from the records it is quite clear that this tribe had seized at least half of all this land in a short period of time, from 1825 to 1850, and while they claimed it all by right of conquest, they had not held it for the long period indicated in their traditions.

Cheyennes and Comanches

From the first, Bent's Fort on the Arkansas River did a profitable trade with the Southern Cheyennes and the Southern Arapahoes. These two tribes, working together, were strong enough to control the buffalo country of western Kansas between the Arkansas and the Platte. They also held much of eastern Colorado. They were such clever horse thieves they always had several extra animals to trade along with their few furs, some buffalo robes, and quantities of dried meat.

As long as these two tribes were in the good graces of the traders at the fort and camped nearby frequently, the Northern Comanches and their allies, the Kiowas and Kiowa Apaches, stayed away. These tribes considered William Bent and his men to be their enemies, for they were so friendly with tribes that raided the Comanche horse herds and on occasion lifted a Comanche scalp. This enmity between the tribes had existed while the Cheyennes were still north of the Platte and grew much stronger after the two northern tribes moved so far south. The Comanches found it difficult to protect their horses against the bold and skillful Cheyennes, some of the best horse thieves in all the Plains.

The intertribal friction finally developed into an all-out war, unlike the usual intertribal hostilities. It began in 1837 when a large band of young Cheyenne warriors organized a raid deep into Oklahoma. They went to the elderly keeper of the sacred arrows of the tribe and asked that he make strong medicine for them, for they were firm believers in securing all the help, both material and spiritual, they could when they were going into such a dangerous country. He refused, saying that he needed more time than they would allow to go through the proper rituals, but they beat him until he agreed and made the medicine, but he warned them that on account of their behavior it would not be strong enough to protect them. The young hotheads would not listen and dashed off to the Comanche pastures where the entire group was attacked and wiped out.

In retaliation for this loss the Cheyennes and Arapahoes gathered all their forces for a massed attack on some Comanche villages to the south of the Arkansas and well downstream. Their preparations for such a large assault required about a year and during that time the medicine men worked hard to build up the strength of the sacred arrows. When all was ready they all went south to Bent's Fort and laid in a large supply of guns and ammunition and went on south, hunting Comanches along the Cimmaron River.

In the first village on their path they found a large party of Northern Comanches whom they took by surprise and won some initial success. The Comanche defenders hastily threw up some earthworks and held their lines against the combined assaults of the aggressors that, contrary to the usual Indian fighting on the Plains, continued throughout the day, with the northern warriors reforming their bands and returning to fight, dashing up in determined charges. At dusk the attackers finally withdrew, having achieved nothing more than a drawn battle after all their preparations and valorous attacks.

But the Comanches had been awed and shaken by the sustained mass attacks of several hundred horsemen, something they had never before encountered in Indian warfare. While they were recovering from the wastage of the battle, William Bent was busy pointing out the great advantages of peace over war in such a situation. Several successful Cheyenne raids on the Comanche horse herds during the period helped strengthen Bent's arguments. Possibly the deciding factor in the affair was an outbreak of smallpox in the Kiowa camp in the winter of 1839–40. Finally the leaders of both groups agreed to meet in a great peace council in the summer of 1840.

A suitable spot for such a large gathering was selected near the Arkansas and a few miles downstream from the post. The Cheyennes and Arapahoes camped on the north bank while the Comanches, Kiowas, and Kiowa Apaches came up and pitched their tipis across the river to the south. The northern contingent arrived first at the grounds. They had stopped at Bent's Fort on their way as they wanted to do some trading in preparation for the big affair. They came into camp burdened with gifts for their expected guests. Meanwhile their hunters levied a heavy toll on the buffalo herds to insure an ample supply of meat for several days of feasting.

After the southerners had come up and pitched camp, the two groups united in several days of feasting, dancing, and exchanging of presents. In return for the lavish piles of goods from the trader's store, the Comanches brought up horses in such numbers that the new owners were hard put to find enough lead ropes for all of them.

After several solemn council meetings and many hours of deliberation the two groups entered into an agreement for a lasting peace, with both groups in firm accord that the Arkansas River henceforth would be the dividing line between the hunting grounds of the tribes. Once the Cheyennes and Arapahoes had been accepted as friends by the Comanches, the latter no longer could accuse William Bent of aiding enemies of their tribe and so they could make a peace with the traders that would develop trade to the benefit of both parties.

Thus the establishment of Bent's Fort on the Arkansas brought a permanent change to the southern Plains, bringing a period of peace to an area where there had been constant fighting. This peace was important to the white men also, for the Santa Fe Trail, by that time a busy highway, traversed the new peaceful zone.

During this same period the establishment of Fort Laramie on the North Platte and the subsequent migration of the Oglalas to the upper Platte had disrupted the pattern for the entire area surrounding the new post. While this migration had eased tensions in South Dakota east of the Black Hills, it had brought new problems to the Platte country. In a short time new wars between the various tribes broke out, triggered by the presence of the newcomers. In both of these instances it was the intervention of the outsiders, the white traders, that had caused the changes. Many more disruptions of the old patterns on the Plains followed in the next few years, all of them caused in a large part, or entirely, by the westward-moving whites.

As the interference by the whites became more pronounced and more irritating, the various tribes found their old intertribal wars of less and less immediate importance. Instead they turned their attention more to blocking the westward flow of the settlers, and in a few years old enemies were uniting in attacks against this common foe. This shift is so pronounced that after about 1850 almost all the movements of Indian tribes were the direct results of white actions, and increased at an accelerating pace until all the nomadic hunters of the Plains were confined to reservations, sometimes far from their old tribal homes.

13

The Great Council at Fort Laramie

WHEN THE TRAIL TO OREGON WAS OPENED to wagon trains in the early 1840s, the resulting annual flow of travelers brought critical new problems to the Indian tribes along the Platte River, and especially to the Pawnees, Oglalas, Cheyennes, and Arapahoes. As the wagon trains increased in size and number each year, the friction between the travelers and the tribes along the trail soon built up to the danger point and minor conflicts erupted all along the way. Most of the problems between red men and white resulted directly from the whites' ignorance concerning Indian customs and practices, coupled with the white man's firm belief that an Indian had no rights of any kind, even in his own land.

From the Indian point of view the whites were invaders on Indian lands, unwanted and uninvited. Initially they came in small groups with horses, mules, and cattle, all desirable to the Indians, and to be had for the taking. Their wagons were loaded with goods such as clothes, blankets, steel tools, iron kettles, and the like, and usually carried a large supply of food. And to top it off most of the whites were frightened when any Indians approached. Their fear often caused them to act in a foolish manner, giving the Indians an added advantage. The frightened whites considered the Indian warriors as dangerous wild animals and, according to the immediate situation, to be driven away or killed if they were not too strong. If they were strong, they should be bribed with presents of food and clothing.

To the Indians it was obvious that these enemies on tribal lands were doing the red men a great deal of harm. They killed off or frightened away the buffalo herds along the entire length of the Platte Valley. Their livestock ate off grass needed for game and for the Indian horses. Their campsites and litter despoiled the countryside. They took potshots at friendly Indians, seemingly for no reason at all, and looked scornfully at any of the red men who came to visit their camps. They were rude intruders in foreign country without permission and unaware of that fact.

In such a situation it is understandable that the Indians gathered in and kept any stray livestock, and often disturbed the pasturing or sleeping herds at night to encourage more straying. They surrounded and plundered small parties of helpless travelers they met along the trail. Indeed it is a mystery why the Indians under such circumstances were so tolerant and why serious incidents were so few. One of the more serious incidents could occur when an Indian war party found a wagon train at a disadvantage and could make a dash for the herd of loose stock as in this raid, recorded by Francis Parkman.[1]

> They had encamped by the side of the Platte, and their oxen were scattered over the meadows, while the horses were feeding a little farther off. Suddenly the ridges were alive with a swarm of mounted Indians, at least six hundred in number, who came pouring with a yell down toward the camp. . . . suddenly wheeling, they swept toward the band of horses, and in five minutes had disappeared with their prey. . . .

In 1849 the problems along the trail multiplied rapidly as a horde of forty thousand excited gold seekers on their way to California swarmed up the Platte, all of them rushing by in a period of about six weeks. They had left one or another of the small towns on the Missouri River in early May as soon as the new growth of prairie grass was long enough to feed their draft animals. The first of the trains reached the Platte Valley about the first of June, and for all of that month filled the bottom lands with scarcely a gap between successive wagon trains. At night the river bottom was an almost unbroken line of camps, their fires flickering in the dark while thousands of animals devoured every blade of grass for miles back from the river bank. Along this trail the buffalo herds a few years earlier had been so large and numerous that at times they were nuisances, or even a real danger as this brief passage from a journal in 1839 shows.[2] This caravan had decided to travel until midnight in order to reach a good camping spot, but found their way obstructed by sleeping buffalo.

> At night their progress was greatly retarded by the herds of buffalo which lined the road and covered the Plain. They were as thick as sheep were ever seen in a field, and moved not until the caravan was within ten feet of them. They would then rise and flee at random, greatly affrighted, and snorting and bellowing to the equal alarm of the horses and mules.

But in the summer of 1849 all the buffalo herds were soon chased off to the south for twenty miles or more by the eager greenhorn hunters who sometimes had difficulty finding their way back to camp. Even after the trains had all passed, the valley lay desolate and dusty under the scorching midsummer sun, a trodden waste several miles wide, an effective barrier to any herds wanting to use the river as a watering place.

While the Pawnees claimed the land on both sides of the Platte River near its mouth, and the Oglalas held the whole of the North Platte above the forks, there was still a long stretch between these two tribes open to any roving band from any tribe, and here a train might encounter Pawnees, Cheyennes, Arapahoes, Oglalas, or Brulés. Some of these mounted parties were just hunters, but more often they were war parties out for a little excitement and any loot that might come their way, especially stray horses or cattle, or a small group of unwary travelers that might be plundered with impunity. These warriors had no feeling of guilt whatever in plundering these intruders even when the warriors were far from their own land and could not claim they were protecting tribal lands against foreigners. They had no obligation to spare such people unless the specific party had a firm agreement with their tribe. Any other strangers could be, and usually were, treated as enemies on sight. Of course any travelers so despoiled complained loudly to the commander of the nearest army post and demanded protection against those fierce Indians, with the return of their property if it could be found.

While the great rush of 1849 was still at its height, the whole Indian problem was removed from the jurisdiction of the Department of War and placed as a bureau under the newly created Department of Interior. The Indian Bureau then decided to try a new approach to the

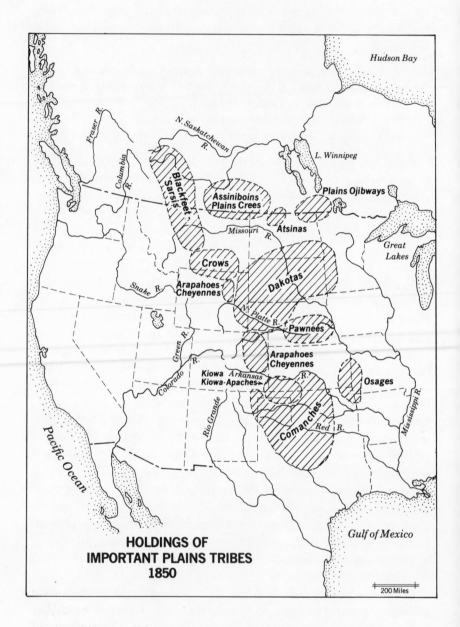

Hudson Bay

Fraser R.

N. Saskatchewan R.

L. Winnipeg

Columbia R.

Blackfeet-Sarsis

**Assiniboins
Plains Crees**

Plains Ojibways

Missouri R.

Atsinas

Great Lakes

Crows

Dakotas

Snake R.

Arapahoes-Cheyennes

N. Platte R.

Pawnees

Green R.

**Arapahoes
Cheyennes**

Colorado R.

**Kiowa
Kiowa-Apaches**

Arkansas R.

Osages

Rio Grande

Comanches

Red R.

Mississippi R.

Pacific Ocean

Gulf of Mexico

**HOLDINGS OF
IMPORTANT PLAINS TRIBES
1850**

200 Miles

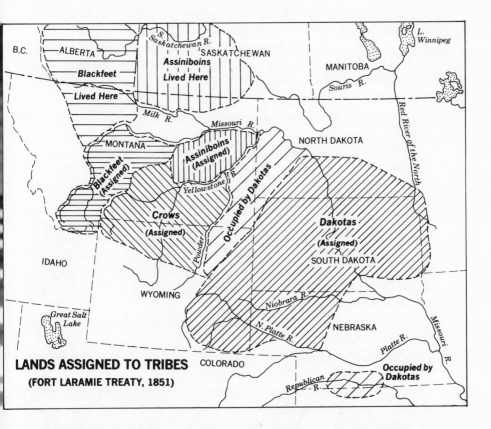

LANDS ASSIGNED TO TRIBES
(FORT LARAMIE TREATY, 1851)

whole Indian problem in the West in an effort to make the main trails west safer to the many travelers.

Since most of the problems between the travelers and the Indians arose when the whites met the roving war parties seeking spoils of war and honors in an enemy area, any plan that would cut down on these wide-ranging war parties would ease the problem all along the trails. To secure the active cooperation of all the tribes involved, it was necessary to talk with all of them in a common council and bind each tribe to the government and to each other with a body of treaties.

The first step then was to convene a great council at some central place, such as Fort Laramie on the North Platte. There a large camp was set up to hold all the visitors and many wagon loads of supplies were freighted in from the Missouri. All this was a few miles downriver from the fort where there was ample room for hundreds of tipis and pasturage for thousands of horses. This spot was far enough from the fort that the camp litter would be no problem later, and the grass near the post would be saved for the company horses. To conduct this large operation the Indian Bureau chose an old fur trader and mountain man, Thomas Fitzpatrick, and a wise choice that proved to be. He knew the Indians and their problems, and equally important, the Indians knew and trusted him, for he had traded with all the tribes over the years.

When the council finally assembled there were several thousand Indians present, all guests of the United States and feasting on white man's food brought in by wagon trains from the east. To no one's surprise, the Oglalas who claimed possession of all the land for many miles around made up most of the group, more than all the rest put together. Several of the Plains tribes were convinced beforehand that the Oglalas would be present in such numbers that it would be dangerous for any delegation from a hostile tribe to appear, even though Fitzpatrick had the assurance of the Oglala leaders that they would remain peaceful.

There were no leaders from either the Southern Cheyenne or the Southern Arapaho tribes, for these two had been at outs with the Oglalas since 1834 over the land between the forks of the Platte. However, both the Northern Cheyennes and the Northern Arapahoes came in appreciable numbers. They lived to the north as buffers between the Oglalas and the Crows and sometimes these three tribes joined against the Crows in an attempt to drive the latter from the Powder River country. Small delegations came from the Wind River Shoshonis and from their neighbors, the Crows. Both of those tribes wanted support from the council against the intruding Oglalas and Tetons menacing them from the east. The Arickaras, by now only a weak remnant of a once proud people, sent a few men from central North Dakota. The Atsinas and Assiniboins from along the Canadian border had delegations, and there must have been a few Blackfeet, for the tribe was mentioned in the treaty.

After the preliminary speeches had been given, the council turned at once to the problem of the tribal lands. Each tribe was asked to describe its holdings and to set its boundaries, with the other tribes ready to object to any encroachment. The only serious objections to any of the claims came from the Crows when the Oglalas boldly claimed ownership of the upper Powder River drainage which they had seized a few years earlier. The Crows testified that they had held that land for over a hundred years, but their claim was ignored.

After all the tribal claims had been made, the boundaries of the lands were described.[3] A map drawn according to these descriptions looks odd indeed when one considers the positions of the tribes at that time. Although the Oglalas had been disputing with the Cheyennes and Arickaras for about fifteen years over the triangle of land between the forks of the Platte, they allowed all of it to be given to those two tribes, seemingly without a protest.

The Crow boundaries were described as starting at the mouth of the Powder River and extending up that stream, then across to the source of the Yellowstone River, and down that stream to the mouth of Twenty-five Yard (Shield's) River, then north to the Musselshell River and east along that stream until it turns north. From there the Crow boundary went directly south to the Yellowstone and on down to the starting place. The Crows objected, for they wanted the east side of the Powder River Valley as well, as far as the watershed of the Little Missouri.

As the line for the Oglalas was drawn from about Casper, Wyoming, to the head of Heart River in North Dakota, the whole Little Missouri was left as a buffer between the Oglalas and the Crows, but the Oglalas went right out and occupied all of the Little Missouri Valley and tried to take the eastern half of Powder River Valley.

The Assiniboins, who lived well to the north of the Missouri River along the Canadian border were given the triangle of land between the Missouri and the Yellowstone as far west as the Musselshell, and nothing to the north of the Missouri where they lived, an allotment difficult to understand.

The land assigned to the Blackfeet, except for the Judith Basin, was entirely out of Blackfeet country, all of it south of the Missouri while the Blackfeet actually owned the country from the Missouri north to the Canadian line.

It is evident that the treaty council had little concern over setting accurate boundaries. What the commissioners really wanted was the right to keep the Oregon Trail open for the travelers, with a few army posts along the way, ostensibly to protect the Indians from the whites, but really to protect the whites from the Indians. These items were granted by the chiefs, and they promised to keep their young men within the tribal boundaries in the future.

The Oglalas broke the treaty within a month or so. A large band moved southeast into the upper Republican Fork in Kansas and stayed there for several years, fighting with the Pawnees at frequent intervals. For a time they eased up in their efforts to drive the Crows out of the Powder River country. Although the Oglalas, Cheyennes, and Arapahoes sent out war parties each year against the Crows, the Powder River country enjoyed a few peaceful seasons. A hunting enthusiast from England, Sir St. George Gore, with Jim Bridger as his guide and director of his expedition, hunted the entire year, 1855–56, on the Powder River and had no Indian trouble whatever.

14

The Comanches: 1785-1855

THE COMANCHES on the southern Plains soon recovered from their smallpox losses. They went out and captured a few hundred more women to help in the production of the babies. They resumed their customary activities of raiding and horse stealing. Although the tribe was steadily increasing in size, it did not move out to occupy new lands because it was hemmed in on two sides by natural barriers and on the other two by strong opponents. To the west and southwest the desert stretched far, its desert scrub and very scanty grass offering unsuitable pasturage for either buffalo or horses and so of no interest to the nomadic Comanches. To the south in Texas were the Spanish settlements that might be raided with little danger to the warriors, but they could not be wiped out by the erratic Comanches who really did not want that farming country to live in. All the war parties against the settlements could accomplish in the long run was to blunt any attempts at western expansion of the farmlands. To the east and north of the Comanches were strong tribes, well armed and well organized, capable of holding their lands indefinitely against the nomads.

Thus while the Blackfeet on the far northern Plains and the Dakotas off to the northeast were expanding their frontiers until their holdings had doubled or tripled, the Comanches were kept busy just holding on to what they had. An important factor here was the inability of the

Comanches to weld their scattered bands into any sort of disciplined unity. The Comanches roamed about in numerous small bands united to one another only by a common language and a common culture. During this entire period they never all came together in a common council to discuss common problems and courses of action. They never produced a great leader capable of uniting several of the bands for a period of years and acting in a common cause.

During the period 1785–1805 the Comanches were busy in southern Texas, staging many small raids on the Spanish settlers on the western edge of the colony. These poor people were not allowed to own guns for their own protection. The soldiers in the small garrisons scattered thinly about the colony were expected by the authorities to beat off all enemy attacks. However, these soldiers were poorly armed, poorly supplied, and too often poorly led, a sorry condition brought on by the weakness of Spain and that country's embroilment in the European struggles of the period.

The Comanches were quite willing to take advantage of this weakness. In addition to attacking the outlying areas and capturing or killing the people, the raiding bands often had a period of peaceful activity during which they visited the larger settlements demanding and receiving presents that would insure their continuing friendship. Often some of these Comanche bands were friendly for a few years, but other bands not present at the peace council felt no obligation to keep any promises made by their brethren and continued raiding. Hence each year the colonists suffered severe losses of livestock, sometimes even at the hands of the departing friends who had just been feasted and furnished with what poor goods the colonists could produce.

The troubles in Texas increased after the United States acquired the Louisiana Territory in 1803. While Spain governed Louisiana some effort was made by the officials to keep the traders along the Mississippi River from supplying guns and ammunition to the Plains tribes, and horses were not allowed free passage from Texas to the markets around New Orleans. After the Anglo-Americans took possession of Louisiana they occupied the small trading posts along the old border between Louisiana and Texas and sent traders up the rivers to trade directly with buffalo-hunting Indians, especially the Wichitas who were happy to buy quantities of guns from the traders and pass them along to the Comanches in exchange for horses stolen from southern Texas or northern Mexico. Also several of the Americans were not averse to raiding Texas herds themselves, pretending that their loot really consisted of wild horses captured out on the unsettled Plains.

Although the Wichitas and the Comanches had a common boundary and some conflict of interest over portions of the buffalo country, they remained on peaceful terms to maintain the trade which produced a profit for both tribes. The Osages who lived on to the north of the Wichitas did not make any formal peace agreement with the Comanches, but they were still able to do a good trade in Comanche horses by letting other Indians to the north of the Comanches act as middlemen. Horses traded to the Wichitas usually were sent on east to the Mississippi River crossing at Natchez, or downriver to the plantations of lower Louisiana, while the Osages supplied the Midwest markets by sending horses through St. Louis and across into the Ohio Valley.

The Comanches were careful to preserve both of these outlets, for they needed to trade off several thousand horses each year, many more than could be absorbed by their immediate neighbors. They could not trade the animals to the north, for that way was blocked by hostile tribes who secured their share of the Comanche herds by theft instead of trade. Although the trading posts in New Mexico were available and welcomed the Comanche trade, their stock of goods, especially of guns, was limited and their prices were high.

The Spanish settlements in southern Texas continued to weaken, a side result of the prolonged Napoleonic Wars in Europe. The settlers were under heavy attacks each year from the Comanches with their new guns purchased through the Wichitas, and were driven back until the Comanches dominated the Colorado Valley and its superior buffalo-hunting grounds. At this time, about 1800–10, the Comanche holdings reached their greatest extent. Although for many years after that they fought strongly against all encroachments on what they regarded as their lands, they were gradually pushed back along the southern, eastern, and northern borders during the next fifty years. Only to the southwest were the Comanches free from any real threat. There they still fought once in a while with the dwindling Lipan Apaches, but that tribe was too small to drive the Comanches back, and the waste lands beyond them were of no interest to the mounted nomads. The Utes and Apaches along the western borders often dashed out into the buffalo country in small hunting bands, retreating hastily once they had secured some meat, for they were anxious to avoid any serious fighting with their fierce neighbors.

When Mexico secured its independence from Spain in 1821 and Texas was no longer under the burdensome Spanish rule, the Mexican officials allowed Anglo-Americans to acquire land and build settlements along the western borders of the farming lands of the old settlers, to act as a buffer against the Comanche raiders. These newcomers were tough, hardy men, many of them from the southern Appalachians. They suffered a great deal from the raiders, but they fought back at every opportunity and were able to blunt the Comanche attacks and keep down the losses in livestock. More importantly, they secured control of the trade of horses into Louisiana, and so cut deeply into the Comanche-Wichita trade.

The Comanches suffered the loss of thousands of horses each year to thieves from the northern tribes, with the Crows and Cheyennes being rated as the cleverest of all. They still had about twenty thousand animals to trade and could offer them in large lots, attracting buyers from many places. Intermittently they still had good trade relations with the Osages between outbursts of fighting. Whenever the two tribes were actively attacking each other, the Osages could still get Comanche horses by turning to the Kiowas and Cheyennes as middlemen, but in any case the trading went on each year, for the Comanches wanted plenty of trade goods, especially the guns and ammunition that the Osages secured in abundance from the American traders.

After American traders from St. Louis opened the Santa Fe Trail across to New Mexico, they were in close contact with the northern Comanche bands, for the trail had to pass through tribal lands for about three hundred miles. The traders and Comanches found it to their mutual advantage to maintain peaceful relations in the interest of trade, in addition to a safe passage for the merchants. Although small Indian bands did raid the trains from time to time, most of these were by parties of horse thieves from tribes far to the northwest, especially the Northern Arapahoes, and even an occasional band of Blackfeet from the Glacier Park region.

Not long after the opening of the Santa Fe Trail, William Bent built Bent's Fort on the Arkansas River and in a few years brought about the big peace council of 1840 that ended the warfare between the northern tribes and the Northern Comanches, an event discussed in some detail previously. In this agreement the Comanches gave up all claims to a large strip of land in western Kansas north of the Arkansas River.

On the northeastern border of the Comanche hunting grounds the Osages and the Caddoan tribes along the Red River sent large parties of hunters each year into the buffalo country for meat. The Comanches were unhappy about this state of affairs but they endured it in order to preserve their trade of stolen horses for Wichita guns, although they did try to confine the hunters to a strip of land near the eastern edge of the Plains.

Then in the 1830s this problem of encroachment from the east grew into serious proportions. The Indian Bureau, at that time under the War Department, began moving tribes from the Carolinas, Georgia, and Tennessee into Indian Territory, now Oklahoma. All of these Indians were fairly well organized and they had very good guns. Soon they took over Comanche lands. Thus all along the eastern and northern front the Comanches were pushed back, resulting in a net loss, for there was no other land near that they could annex.

As the eastern Indian tribes continued to move west, usually under prodding from the War Department, the bands of hunters west of the Mississippi increased in numbers until they were able to take over some of eastern Kansas. These new tribes had never hunted buffalo on the Plains in earlier years so the only way they could find room to hunt was to encroach on the Plains tribes.

On they came, Delawares, Shawnees, Seminoles, Cherokees, and Kickapoos, until the Plains tribes decided to resort to forceful measures to drive them back. One summer in the early 1850s the Plains tribes along the Arkansas River gathered a large number of their fighting men into a striking force of fifteen hundred mounted warriors armed with bows, arrows, lances, and a few guns. This unlikely mixture of friends and enemies from the Cheyennes, Arapahoes, Kiowas, Kiowa Apaches, Comanches, and Osages, and quite probably a scattering of young men from several other tribes but on their own, just looking for action, set out to sweep the alien hunters from the Plains. A picked force of the finest warriors of the Plains went forth searching for intruders. What force of Indians could withstand them?

After a short search they found about a hundred Sauks and Foxes out hunting. These intruders took one look at the formidable array of enemies and scurried to the nearest shelter, a small ravine. Here they crouched, ready to shoot down any horsemen that ventured too close.

The warriors dashed about on their horses while the little band picked them off at long range with their fine rifles, safe from any counterfire from all the enemy guns except a few good rifles in the hands of the Osages. The attackers finally retreated in confusion and dismay after suffering severe losses. The Sauks and Foxes lost only six, all to the Osage rifles. Thus ended the greatest organized intertribal effort on the southern plains to beat back the encroaching tribes from the east.

15

The End of an Era

THE BIG INDIAN COUNCIL at Fort Laramie in 1851 led
directly to important changes in the Indian Bureau's handling of Indian
affairs. It brought to an end the migration of Indian tribes and fixed the
pattern of future Indian reservations. After the tribes had established
their boundary claims and had signed treaties at Fort Laramie
promising to stay within those boundaries, the government officials
induced the other tribes to do likewise. In each big treaty council the
officials usually accepted the tribal claims as presented, then asked each
tribe to sell some of the marginal land in return for annual payments in
goods and services. The land not ceded was then reserved for the tribe
and soon became known as the tribal reservation. Each tribe in turn
promised in the treaty to stay within its own boundaries as set in the
council. This program brought an end to Indian migrations. No longer
could a tribe at its own volition move to new lands. From this time on
it moved only at the direction and under the supervision of the
government officials.

Thus the last large relocation of Plains Indians was not a migration
in the old style but the forceful removal of the remnants of the Santee
Dakotas from the Minnesota country in 1862 following the bloody
Sioux war of that summer. When the Santee bands, numbering about
seven thousand people, were driven from their farms by the soldiers,

they were forced to take up a nomadic existence on the Plains to the west until they could be resettled on reservation lands. For a hundred years after the Dakotas had acquired horses, this large portion of the Dakotas had clung tenaciously to their little villages and finally gave up their homes and farms only under duress.

Of all the seminomadic tribes living along the eastern fringe of the Plains or along the Missouri River, not a single one of its own accord cut loose from their villages and farms to become entirely nomadic. The Cheyennes were the only Indians among all of these to make the transition before the coming of the white settlers, and they took that course only after having been driven from their various farming villages four times in about fifty years—first from the valley of the Minnesota River, then from the Lake Traverse area, from the Sheyenne River valley in North Dakota, and finally from the banks of the Missouri.

On the western side of the Plains there were the Apaches who, of their own accord, tried for years to change from being nomadic hunters to being small farmers who went out hunting. They came down from Canada into western Kansas in small hunting bands, seemingly quite successful as hunters, but they then began to build villages with small earth lodges and to plant some crops. They had progressed to the point where they could be classed as seminomadic before they were driven out. This pattern of behavior on the part of the Apaches is of some significance here for during the period of this change they were in the heart of the buffalo country where the hunting was very good.

The tribes that became nomadic horsemen by choice were those from the west and north where they had done no farming of any kind within the recent past, with the exception of the Crows who raised a little tobacco in the Yellowstone Valley. The other tribes were the Comanches from the Colorado mountains, the Wind River Shoshonis from the Great Basin, the Kiowas from the upper Missouri, the Kiowa Apaches, Sarsis, Blackfeet, Assiniboins, Atsinas, Arapahoes, Plains Crees, and Plains Ojibways, all from the north.

By the time these nomadic tribes were finally placed on reservations, several of them were approaching a seminomadic status, for they had found it expedient to establish winter camps, separating into small bands in order to insure forage for the horses, but staying within a few miles of each other for company for about three months each winter.

Such winter camps have been mentioned specifically as the customary pattern for the Kiowas, Crows, Wind River Shoshonis, and Blackfeet, and probably were used by several of the other tribes. The Crows usually built a few log cabins at each camp. It is evident from the pattern of these camps that none of these tribes moved around during the winter months unless faced with some immediate problem. They easily might have developed their winter camps into villages if their entire life-style and culture had not been drastically changed by the coming of the white man.

Without the guns and horses brought to North America from Europe, the peopling of the Great Plains would have been a much slower development, with very few of the tribes becoming nomadic hunters. Without horses for transportation in the wide open spaces of the Plains the people would surely have continued to live along the streams in little farming villages in the pattern of the Pawnees and Wichitas.

From the first introduction of horses to the Plains, the entire life-style of all the buffalo-hunting tribes was changed and the cultures of all of them were in a state of flux. In a span of somewhat less than two centuries, from 1680 to 1850, there had been continuing drastic changes and a constant reshuffling of tribes and tribal boundaries. The rate of change had increased with each passing decade, leaving the tribesmen in a disturbed state. The older members of the tribes were helpless in their attempts to combat the new ways. Cholera, measles, smallpox, and other diseases took a heavy toll among them, opening the way for the younger people to speed the innovations. Cultural borrowings between the tribes kept pace with the economic changes dictated by the increased reliance on the trader and his wares, but as the Indian's demands for the white man's goods increased, he was hard put to find the means of payment for the desired items.

During this period of change and unrest the Plains tribes were well off for food, clothing, and shelter, but they were very poor in items of economic value that could be traded for manufactured goods. When the trader displayed his wares they could offer horses in return, but to keep up that trade they had to continually raid ranches far to the south and southwest for new animals, draining a resource that had reached its limits of exploitation.

When steamers came to the upper Missouri in the 1830s, the tribes found that they could sell all the tanned buffalo robes their women could process. Robes for this trade had to come from young cows with the skins taken in the late fall when the winter coats were at their best. The demands for these choice hides led the hunters to slaughter tens of thousands of cows in a few weeks, producing ten to twenty times the amount of meat the tribes could use, so the flayed carcasses were left on the Plains to rot. Also as a result of this selective slaughter in a few years there were a few hundred thousand extra bulls eating off the grass until they died of old age, while the reduction in the number of cows cut heavily into the calf crops of the succeeding years. Under this kind of hunting the buffalo herds were doomed. Each year their numbers dwindled and each year they were crowded into smaller ranges. Later when the white hunters flocked to the buffalo country they but hastened the inevitable end. With the collapse of the buffalo-based economy the whole social and economic structure of the Plains tribes disintegrated.

As early as 1850 this insatiable demand for more trade goods for the tribes was alleviated somewhat by the annual distribution of large quantities of goods by the Indian Bureau agents, acting under the terms of the various treaties, but this relief pushed the tribes another step toward pauperism, and encouraged the individual Indians to delay their adjustment to the changing world.

16

Dog Soldiers among the Tribes

MAN, INHERENTLY A SOCIAL ANIMAL, needs to live in a well-established social group of some sort in order to feel secure. The basic structure in the human social pattern has almost invariably been the family unit, a man, one or more women, and his children, a group dictated on the primitive level by the long period required for a human to develop from a newborn infant to a creature who can survive on his own efforts. These early family groups secured their food from day to day, eating every morsel of anything resembling food as it was found, and continually moving about to new areas each day as the food was exhausted in the old ones.

This pattern was common in many Indian tribes, especially those in the Great Basin, who were still at this level of hunting-gathering when they were finally placed on reservations in the latter part of the nineteenth century. The scanty government required in such a group was provided by the leadership of the dominant male, who was restrained to some extent by the social pressure of his group.

When men learned to unite their efforts to kill the large game animals they soon found they could secure more food and hence enjoy a more ample and secure living if they worked together. Depending on the kind of game hunted, and the general environment in which it was found, the hunting group functioned at its best when it contained from twenty-five to fifty members. Among the buffalo hunters in North America before they secured horses, the group of fifty, containing perhaps ten to twelve adult males and youths old enough to be effective hunters, was the most common and so may be considered as the optimum size for such a group.

Close cooperation among all the various members of the group was necessary if the body was to function efficiently on the hunt. One of them needed to act as a leader, but in such a group seldom could he be domineering. If he is a good leader in the field, his leadership will also be evident in the camp or village, but it will be modified to some extent by the social pressure of the group.

One common factor among all the Plains tribes in later years was the gathering of all the small hunting bands into one large camp for a week or two in early summer. There they visited, traded, held large council meetings, and above all, conducted elaborate religious observances. Such a gathering might contain from a few hundred to a few thousand people. In a camp of that size and made up of several diverse elements, the people could not depend on the social pressure of the related groups to maintain order. The young men of the many bands would inevitably gather into informal spontaneous groups to indulge in sports, horseplay, and rowdy play that could easily grow until they disturbed the rest of the camp, or the activities might develop into serious quarreling if the tendency was not checked at an early stage.

All the Plains tribes, except the Comanches, developed groups of young men to act as police during the encampment. Although all of them lived in a similar Plains environment and centered their activities around the buffalo herds, it is probable that the strong similarities in their police organizations and the customs governing them resulted more from their having stemmed from a common source.

The leading candidate for this common source is the Siouan family of tribes that lived in the Ohio Valley for centuries, and later furnished twelve of the twenty-seven Plains tribes and at least half the total population. By 1680 they occupied the eastern edge of the Plains from the Missouri-Kansas border north to Lake Winnipeg in Manitoba, except for one small segment in southern Minnesota held by the Cheyennes of the Algonkin family. In addition two more Siouan tribes, the Kansas and the Mandans, had villages on the Missouri River. The Dakotas alone furnished about one-fourth of the total population at that time, while the two other large tribes of later years, who were not Siouan, the Blackfeet and the Comanches, had not even reached the Plains. Hence it is quite probable that the preponderance of Siouan tribes had a strong influence on the cultural developments of the Plains area.

In the Ohio Valley the culture of the tribes of the Siouan family had definitely reached a higher level than that of the Athapascans coming from the forests of northern Canada, or the Algonkins from the woodlands north of the Great Lakes, or the Shoshonis of the Great Basin. It is probable that the Caddoan family, containing among others the Pawnees and Wichitas, was at about the same level of development as the Siouan family. The Caddoans contributed religious rites involving Sun worship while the Dakotas probably brought in both the pattern for the tribal police and the war game complex.

Both the Siouan and Caddoan families had large agricultural settlements, massive earthworks, and elaborate religious ceremonies. They also had settled populations, some sort of political control, and police forces both to keep order among the large groups of laborers needed on the large edifices, and to protect the settlements against outside raiders. Thus both the Siouan and Caddoan tribes would carry with them on their migrations some pattern for policing large groups. That their patterns differed somewhat is indicated by the fact that the Siouan tribes depended on social groups for their police while the Pawnees, although they had similar social groups, used religious groups for their police.

The hunting of buffalo, even by woodland groups who had only the very small herds scattered in the forest glades as their prey, required the united efforts of all the hunters in the vicinity of the herd. One strong tendency of buffalo is for the herd to run far away from danger once they become frightened. They will move quickly for twenty miles or more before settling down again in new pastures. A single hunter creeping up on a herd might easily put it to flight and ruin the buffalo hunting in his area for several weeks.

Tribes that hunted buffalo in the woodland fringe soon felt the need for some control over these single hunters that would effectually prevent the disturbing of the game at unsuitable times. The social controls used on such hunters by the Dakotas were patterned on those developed in the large farming settlements in the Ohio Valley and adapted to the smaller frontier communities. An early report on such a control group was written by Father Hennepin when he visited a Dakota village on the Mississippi River headwaters in 1680.

> Fifteen or sixteen savages came into the middle of the place where they were, with their great clubs in their hands. The first thing they did was to overset the cabin of those that had invited us. Then they took away all their victuals and what bears oil they could find in the bladders, or elsewhere, with which they rubbed themselves all over from head to foot. . . . We knew not what these savages were at first, but it appear'd they were some of those we had left above the Falls of St. Anthony. One of them, who called himself my uncle, told me that those who had given us victuals, had done basely to go and forestal the others in the chase; and according to the laws and customs of their country, 'twas lawful for them to plunder them, since they had been the cause that the Bulls were all run away, before the nation could get together, which was a great injury to the publick; for when they are all met, they make a great slaughter amongst the Bulls; for they surround them on every side, that 'tis impossible for them to escape.

After the Dakotas moved out onto the Plains and became nomadic hunters they continued this same pattern of control. A band of young men, organized as one of the social groups of the tribe, was appointed to keep the peace in the camp, and usually the same group was in charge of the buffalo hunts. While the Anglo-Europeans sometimes called such men camp police, more often they were known as Dog Soldiers, for these groups often took such names as Dogs, Little Dogs, or Crazy Dogs.

The Mandan and Hidatsa villages on the Missouri were friendly toward white visitors and were easily reached by steamboat from 1832 on. Interested observers, including painters, were welcome to attend the ceremonies of the social groups and to follow their program of duties. Hence a great deal of detailed observation, amplified by sketches drawn on the spot, is in the records on the social activities of these two tribes. Among the Mandans the society of young men known as the Black Mouths had the task of policing tribal activities whether in the village, on the hunt, on the march, or at a Sun Dance ceremony.

Among the Mandans, Hidatsas, Blackfeet, Arapahoes, and Atsinas, when a boy reached the age of about twelve, he felt he was ready to belong to the lowest-ranking social group. He and all his friends who had not been quite old enough to join on the previous occasion about three years earlier banded together and sought the aid of their parents and relatives for their venture. Although there were no set age limits for this group of boys, all of the older boys of the tribe, fifteen or older, had already joined, and the boys under twelve were considered too young so the group was made up entirely of boys from about twelve to nearly fifteen years old, and because of the structure of the social groups in the tribe and their arrangement in a "ladder" form, each of the ten groups in turn was made up of boys or men who were about the same age, and averaged some three years older than the next lower group on the "ladder."

The boys then with the help of their parents and relatives gathered a large quantity of desirable articles until they finally had enough to satisfy the demands of the boys in the lowest-ranking society who then traded to them all their regalia, songs, dances, etc., for the pile of goods. In addition the younger boys had to feast the older boys for four nights. The older boys then were without any social group of their own so they took the pile of goods, added some more to it, and purchased the next higher-ranking society. This process continued until at the end the highest-ranking society, containing a group of men about fifty years old, sold out and retired with their large pile of wealth to be divided among them. The whole process was repeated every few years and a boy could climb from the foot to the head of the ladder in thirty-five to forty years if he were fortunate enough to live that long.

While each of these societies, ten in all among the Mandans, had its place in the social life of the tribe and had a list of specified activities and ceremonies to conduct, one of them, about the fourth up the ladder, had the specific additional duty of acting as the police force during the entire year. Among the Mandans this duty fell to the Black Mouths. Since this group contained all the young men of the tribe of any consequence in a certain age group, and had the strong support of the entire tribe, composed as it was of their own close relatives, it was able to enforce all the tribal rules and regulations with very little friction or resistance.

In the other Plains tribes the corresponding Dog Soldier society was of equal importance. Supported by public opinion, the members were the only men who could act as a group in their official capacity to discipline a noted warrior or chief without meeting determined resistance from that proud man who could submit to them without suffering total public disgrace. If he resisted, he would be in much deeper disgrace for his resistance to duly constituted authority than he would have been for his misdeed and punishment.

Similar societies, but not founded on age groups, were prominent among the Dakotas, Assiniboins, Crows, Cheyennes, Pawnees, and Arickaras, and in those tribes were assigned the duties of keeping the peace and supervising the hunts. While the Mandans, living in large permanent villages, needed their Black Mouths the year round, the Crows needed their Dog Soldiers only for the summer season when the tribe gathered in the large summer encampment. When the time and place for the meeting had been decided, the recognized leader who had been chosen as head of the camp appointed one of the four societies—Foxes, Lumpwoods, Big Dogs, or Muddy Hands—to take charge of the police duties for the summer. They were to supervise the communal buffalo hunts, keep peace in the camp, halt any war parties that tried to start out on inauspicious occasions, and act as peacemakers in general in calming small disturbances.

A good account of the Crow Dog Soldiers in action was given by an old-time trader who lived with the Crows for a time when he was a young man.[1] It was at the time of the great summer encampment and the few hundred tipis were pitched on the bottom land near the river. This young man and two of his Crow friends, all like-minded rascals looking for some excitement and devilment, decided it would be great fun to run a small band of buffalo through the camp during a quiet morning. Since the camp was a large one and extended for a mile or so along the stream, all the mischief-makers had to do was to find a small band of buffalo feeding on the bench possibly a mile or two away. Those buffalo might then be stampeded down one of the draws and once the herd was underway there would be no way to stop them or turn them aside.

When the fleeing animals dashed out onto the river bottom from the draw they were right in the midst of the tipis with everyone dashing about in a panic. Before the startled animals could break free they had run through a few tipis, knocking them down and tearing the hide covers. They also overturned a few racks of drying meat and scattered cooking fires. Fortunately no one was injured, but several of the women were most unhappy. The camp police rounded up the pranksters in short order and meted out the punishment. In addition to paying for the damaged tipis, the three were sentenced to a month's banishment from the encampment, which meant they had to miss all the fun and games, the visiting and feasting. They obeyed at once and left camp lest they might be flogged, and hid out back in the hills a few miles away.

Their womenfolk mitigated their punishment somewhat by sneaking out a few times at night to console them and to bring them some cooked food. Fortunately for these women they were not caught at this or they surely would have suffered for it. In this instance the punishment was much lighter than what would have been given to a person disturbing the buffalo herds when the tribe was planning a big hunt. That sort of misbehavior endangered the food supply for the entire tribe, and would have brought a severe public flogging and the breaking of the culprit's weapons. If he had killed an animal, the meat from it would have been confiscated and given to other people.

A rather common breach of the peace in an Indian encampment or village was the loud quarreling between two angry women. If the two did not calm down when warned, their punishment was severe and immediate. Meriwether Lewis observed such an incident in an Arickara village on the Missouri. The Arickaras had peace officers who served throughout the year as did the Mandan Black Mouths, although among the Arickaras these men belonged to a religious rather than to a social group.

> While on shore today we witnessed a quarrel between two squaws, which appeared to be growing every moment more boisterous, when a man came forward, at whose approach everyone seemed terrified and ran. He took the squaws and without any ceremony whipped them severely. On inquiring into the nature of such summary justice we learnt that this man was an officer well known to this and many other tribes. His duty is to keep the peace, and the whole interior police of the village is confided to two or three of these officers, who are named by the chief and remain in power for some days. . . . his power is supreme, and in the suppression of any riot or disturbance no resistance to him is suffered . . . their distinguishing mark is a collection of two or three raven skins fixed to the girdle behind the back in such a way that the tails stick out horizontally from the body. On his head, too, is a raven skin split into two parts and tied so as to let the beak project from the forehead.[2]

Among the Blackfeet the punishment for disturbing the buffalo herd sometimes was quite light, with no flogging of the culprit or the breaking of his weapons. This incident observed first hand by David Thompson illustrates this point.[3]

The same evening a Chief walked through the camp informing them that as the bisons were too far off for the hunting party they had given orders to the Soldiers to allow no person to hunt until further notice. Such an order was sure to find some tents ill provided. While we were there, hunting was forbidden on this account. Two tents which had gambled away their things, even to dried provisions, had to steal a march on the soldiers under pretense of looking after their horses, but finding they did not return were watched. In the evening of the second day they approached the camp, with their horses loaded with meat which the Soldiers seized, and the owners quickly gave up; the former distributed the meat to the tents that had many women and children, and left nothing to the owners; but those that had received the meat, in the night sent them a portion of it. Not a murmur was heard, every one said they had acted right.

Seemingly in this instance the camp as a whole had an adequate supply of meat and no large hunt was planned for a few days. Also it is implied, since the case was not considered more serious, that the herds had not been greatly disturbed by the actions of these hunters. On a similar occasion among the Blackfeet about half a century later the Dog Soldiers broke the culprit's weapons, tore his clothing, damaged his saddle, cut his rope and whip into bits, and left him in sad shape. It is evident that in any tribe the punishment might vary a great deal, but always the meat was confiscated, and usually the weapons were broken and the clothing was torn. The punishment as described by Thompson was the lightest mentioned in any tribe except the Comanches where only public censure was meted out.

It is indicated from a comparison of the punishments used in the various tribes that the severity varied inversely with the wealth of the tribe and the supply of food on hand. A very poor tribe with no food reserves understandably was very angry with anyone whose misconduct brought them all to the verge of starvation.

Most of the tribes subjected the offender to a public whipping and destroyed some of his property. In some tribes the punishment extended to his buffalo horse, which made it a very severe punishment indeed. The Wind River Shoshonis beat the horse about the head, making it head shy and unfit for running buffalo until it could be retrained, a process that might take a few months. ·

In extreme cases among the Cheyennes, especially for a repeat offender, they killed one or more of the culprit's horses, but inflicted no other punishment. The Poncas killed both the horses and dogs, but gave the man some other horses and dogs in a day or so. The Osages and Kansas used only the public flogging. In all these cases the punishment was public and inflicted by the Dog Soldiers.

The severity of the punishment in a poorer tribe is well illustrated by a case in a poverty-stricken band of Atsinas. Their food supply was almost exhausted, but they were hopeful that the buffalo would soon approach closely enough for the hunters to attack them. Here again one of the men went out alone a day or so ahead of time, killed a buffalo, and frightened the herd into running away.

The whole band was greatly disturbed. The Dog Soldiers took the man, confiscated his meat, and gave him a severe flogging in the middle of the camp. Then they broke his bow and arrows and finally led out his buffalo horse to be killed. Thus this poverty-stricken band lost not only its chance for a good supply of meat, but their material resources were seriously reduced by the loss of the weapons and the horse.

Among these primitive bands the people evidently could not envisage a heavy fine as appropriate to the occasion, whereby the weapons and the horse were taken, but instead of being destroyed were used for the benefit of the whole band. Even had they thought of a fine, they had no one to receive the weapons and the horse with the authority to put them to public use.

Although the Atsinas were of Algonkin stock it appears that they had borrowed from their Siouan neighbors, the Mandans and Hidatsas, the pattern of camp police and the type of punishment to be inflicted on such occasions. There is no indication that the Atsinas had any type of camp police before they left the Red River country in Manitoba. Certainly they had no need for such a body while they were still a large number of very small hunting bands scattered through the forests, and the Hidatsas were their closest neighbors once the Atsinas had emerged into the buffalo country.

While the Pawnees in the south also had camp police it is probable that they had brought this practice from the Caddoan settlements in the south, for such large villages as the Caddoans had required some such control. Hence the Pawnees were well entrenched in Nebraska with their own type of organization long before the Mandans, the first of the Siouan tribes, reached the Missouri.

In the Pawnee villages the public flogging of a serious offender could be quite severe. One important leader was beaten so badly that he never fully recovered, although he lived for several years after the flogging. In his case he might have violated some religious rule while he was breaking a camp rule. This would bring him dire punishment, for among the Pawnees the police belonged to a religious society rather than to a social group as was the practice among most of the Plains tribes.

On the southern Plains there was an interesting situation involving the two friendly tribes, the Kiowas and Comanches. Although they were allies and often camped and hunted together, they took quite different approaches to the whole police problem. The Comanches were notorious for having no camp police of any kind. A Comanche warrior would brook no supervision or restraint except in connection with a large-scale buffalo hunt. Even then the supervision was slight and lasted only an hour or so.

The Comanches all admitted that a successful buffalo hunt on a large scale demanded a leader with authority. They managed this by appointing the leader who took office for the morning of the hunt, but no longer. He gathered all the hunters near the herd, arranged them in position, and gave the signal to charge. Once the signal had been given, he was no longer a leader with extra power, but just one of the men.

Among the Kiowas the pattern closely resembled that of the Crows. Their men's societies were similar in membership and duties. The Sun Dance priest of the tribe had the duty of naming one of the men's societies to police the large buffalo hunts and the Sun Dance gatherings. It is apparent that the Kiowas had developed their societies before they moved into the southern Plains for none of the surrounding tribes there had such a pattern. The Kiowas, during their stay of half a century or more near the Black Hills had both the Crows and Mandans as friendly neighbors. Since the Kiowa pattern of men's societies so markedly resembles the patterns of those two tribes, especially that of the Crows, it is evident that they borrowed from that tribe.

The Comanches were quite different from the Kiowas in temperament. It is somewhat surprising that the two had such a long period of friendly relations. The Comanches did very little borrowing of social customs and patterns. Just as they lagged far to the rear of all the other Plains tribes in police matters, they lagged in religious matters, being the very last to adopt a Sun Dance ritual.

A study of the patterns of living among the Plains tribes shows that the kinds of punishment the tribes would accept for their members and could inflict consistently were strictly limited in number. For instance, no Plains tribe gave its Dog Soldiers the authority to inflict physical mutilation, although punishment by mutilation has been common throughout a large part of the world and has been used extensively into modern times. In a number of Plains tribes the mutilation of an erring wife by cutting off the tip of her nose was considered strictly a family affair and was done by the husband at his discretion. In this way he published her shame to the whole tribe. Old photographs show that this punishment was fairly common among the Blackfeet.

It may come as a surprise to most people to learn that murder and other forms of manslaughter committed on a fellow tribesman were considered as private affairs and not as offenses against the tribe. Hence such acts were to be judged and punished by the families of the two persons involved and not by the Dog Soldiers. When any tribe could accept the concept of the blood price wiping out the onus of the deed, many family feuds were prevented, tribal unity was strengthened, and tribal manpower was conserved to be used against tribal enemies.

There were several instances when a killing within the family circle could not be handled in such fashion, usually when a man killed one of his womenfolk. There was no one at hand to exact revenge on him, but if his deed was condemned by the tribe as a whole, he could be exiled from the tribe for a period of five years or more, a severe punishment indeed, for it was difficult for a lone man to survive in the wilds. He usually died at the hands of enemy raiders who counted his scalp at full value.

The two commonest forms of punishment used today in our society, fines and imprisonment, could not be used at all among the nomadic tribes. The collection of fines and the expenditure of the goods thus collected require the services of some public servant. In an evolving society this is first handled by the priests and the fines are in payment for sins.

The whole concept of imprisonment was foreign to the culture of the tribes, and in the case of nomadic tribes would have been impossible to carry out. These Indians had neither the materials nor the craftsmanship to construct a room or a cage to hold a captive indefinitely, nor any method of transporting the culprit and his cage from one camp to another. Even the burden of feeding and guarding the prisoner would severely strain their scanty resources and manpower.

Although slavery was commonly used in many countries as a punishment for a whole list of crimes, among the Plains Indians it was limited to women and children who had committed no crime at all, but had been captured in war. These people usually were traded off or incorporated into the tribe in a year or so. There was nothing in this pattern of slavery to suggest to the Plains Indian that it might be used against a fellow warrior, often a blood relative, to punish him for a breach of the tribal peace. Even had a warrior been enslaved for any cause, it would have been very difficult to hold him in that degraded status, or to get any useful work out of him.

On the whole the rather simple system of Dog Soldiers or camp police to preserve public order worked rather well in a primitive society composed of small, closely integrated units—the bands—where the strong restraining force was the pressure of public opinion. But this sort of control could not keep the peace in larger groups, for the force of public opinion was lessened as the problems became more complex and the ties of blood in the culprit's group often thwarted the efforts of the larger group to punish people who had offended someone outside the blood group. Only the imposition of the reservation system with controls imposed from outside the tribe saved the various tribes from the necessity of developing their tribal governments to handle the larger populations.

17

The Great War Game

THE CONCEPT OF WAR as an activity that should bring glory and honor to the individual, rather than gain territory for a tribe or destroy an enemy people, was common throughout all the Woodland tribes in the Mississippi-Ohio Valley and in the Southeast. Hence when the twelve tribes of the Siouan family and the three of the Caddoan family moved to the Plains they all brought as a part of their cultural heritage this concept and passed it along to the other twelve tribes, along with a rather extensive list of rules to govern the activity.

To the individual Indian in all of these tribes war was always there, to be indulged in at any time he chose. As long as his social group gave him honor and prestige for his war activities, he was addicted to going off to war whenever he was offered the opportunity. During those periods when he was not away seeking glory in distant parts by fighting his many enemies, he had to be on the alert to ward off any like-minded warriors from the other tribes who would surely come several times each year to try to plunder his village and kill him and his family, but he did spend more time and thought on his own forays than on the defense of his home.

Throughout the Plains the many warring bands roving about had foremost in their minds the achievement of glory through accepted accomplishments. They were always seeking loot, preferably horses, and quite frequently they longed for revenge for past wrongs. Hence each raid or foray was complete in itself, and not a part of some long-range program to achieve some desirable change for the tribe, such as the acquisition of new territory.

The scarcity of warfare on a large scale on the Plains stemmed directly from the vast empty spaces that separated the various tribes until recent times. Until the tribes secured horses to aid in their movements, they were too far apart to feel the need of much fighting. In those old days even small-scale raiding was difficult to carry out, for traveling on foot to the enemy village required such a long walk and took many days. Also before the days of horses there was very little loot of enough value to carry all that long, weary way home.

After the Plains became the home of many tribes and they had all increased in population, each tribe began to feel somewhat restricted by its neighbors, but before these conditions could bring on much large-scale warfare for the possession of more land, the epidemic of 1781 had eliminated half the entire population, leaving the various tribes with ample hunting room again. Then about the time they had recovered from the disaster, smallpox again swept the northern Plains in 1837 and staved off any danger of serious overcrowding for a few more years.

Then as the Indians again multiplied and began to feel restless in their crowded lands, the white farmers began encroaching from the east and mining camps filled many of the valleys in the western mountains. This crowding brought on real wars, but by now the Indian hostilities were largely directed against the outsiders rather than against each other. The Indians engaged in more large-scale wars in the period 1850–80 than in all the previous centuries they had been in the buffalo country.

Two fairly large-scale, long-range operations that might be classed as wars if we could just find any evidence of advance planning for them, occurred in the same area between the Platte River and the Arkansas. These were both made up entirely of small raids that were entirely uncoordinated and were spread out over a period of years and a large area.

In the first war not even the conquest of new territory was a factor in starting the fighting. The Apaches, moving south in several small bands encountered a string of Pawnee villages across their line of advance and over a period of years destroyed them. Then most of them moved on south to set up their own villages.

Hardly had the Apaches gained possession of this area than they were attacked by the Comanches moving from the Colorado mountain valleys. They had horses by that time and were seeking large hunting grounds out on the Plains. In this instance there must have been some awareness among the Comanches that they had to drive out the Apaches if they were to have an adequate share of the buffalo country, but it is extremely doubtful that the Comanches had come down from the mountains with such a clear-cut plan in mind.

On the northern Plains the Blackfeet waged two wars each with the avowed purpose of driving other Indians from some lands desired by the Blackfeet. Between 1785 and 1800 they staged many attacks against the Shoshonis in north central Montana and succeeded in driving them beyond the mountains. Then in the period 1810–37 they waged a war with several planned campaigns, the first designed to destroy the new fur post at Three Forks and thus cut off some of the supply of guns to the enemy Flatheads, the second a much greater effort in 1832 designed to drive the Flatheads and mountain men from all of southwestern Montana and southern Idaho.

A fourth war, of short duration but featuring one pitched battle between forces large enough to be called armies, occurred when the Cheyennes and Arapahoes combined forces to defeat the Northern Comanches south of the Arkansas River in 1838.

These four instances are given to show that the Plains Indians did have some wars that were not just unrelated raids, and to point out the probability that without the white invasion of the Plains on a large scale after 1850 to draw the hostile attentions of many Indian tribes, the Indians would surely have been drawn into full-scale wars against each other in a few more years.

The earlier warfare, consisting almost entirely of raids by small war parties out for glory and honor, had led to the development of an elaborate point scoring system for a warrior's deeds. At the top of the list in most tribes was the counting of the *coup,* a French word meaning blow. Although some of the other war honors vary from tribe to tribe, this one stood above them all, except among the Blackfeet. The classical coup was exemplified by the Cheyennes. A warrior from that tribe dashed at an armed enemy and struck him with a special coup stick, a wand striped like a barber pole, then dashed away to safety. On this rush he carried no weapon in his hand. He needed only to touch some part of the enemy lightly, in the presence of a witness, and then escape with his life to receive this high honor. It seems that a light touch really rated higher than a sharp blow since it indicated a more scornful attitude on the part of the attacker.

A coup of lesser value was scored if a warrior killed an enemy with a weapon held in his hand. In that case three of the warrior's comrades might also count coups of decreasing value by each in turn striking the corpse with a weapon. If a warrior killed a man with an arrow or bullet he could not count coup on the body unless he dashed up and struck it. If one of his comrades could strike the body first, he counted first coup, even though the other man had done the killing.

Among several of the tribes, especially the Teton Dakotas, the taking of an enemy's scalp was rated as a high honor. Since a scalp from any dead enemy, man, woman, or child counted no matter how the victim died, in several instances warriors who lifted the scalps of smallpox victims brought ruin to their own bands when they returned with the infected trophies.

Often a warrior could obtain an enemy scalp by lying in wait near an enemy camp during the night and pouncing on some poor old woman out for water, or a stick of wood, or to relieve herself. Her scalp counted full value in any tribe that gave honors for scalp taking.

Although the common practice in scalping was to remove only the circular patch at the crown, an area about six inches in diameter, some tribes granted the victor the right to all the hair he cared to remove from the victim. An extreme case in the Dakotas was that of a white man who had a heavy crop of curly hair over most of his body. His killer skinned the corpse down to the knees and had his wife tan it for a saddle throw. In contrast with this recognition of scalping, other tribes, for example the Crows, gave no special recognition to scalps although the Crows took them for their victory dances and as souvenirs.

Many tribes gave no special recognition to the stealing of one or more horses from a grazing herd, for this was such an ordinary thing. Cutting loose a horse picketed by a tipi in a camp rated as a high honor. However, it was not enough for the thief to get the horse out of camp. He had to keep it in his possession for a time. One noted Crow warrior stole a very fine horse in the approved manner, but in the ensuing chase lost it again and so could not claim any honor for his theft. The picketed horses were the most sought after, for they were always superior animals such as war horses or buffalo runners, and in the eyes of an Indian raider well worth the extra risk involved. A very fine horse of this type might be worth in trade as much as a hundred ordinary horses.

If a horse was rated very highly by its owner, it was sometimes given extra protection by being brought into the tipi for the night when thieves were expected. This might crowd the tipi to such an extent that two or three of the girls would have to sleep outside, but they were considered to be in little danger of being slain or captured by a man really interested in stealing a superior horse.

Another deed that received a high rating was the snatching of a bow, lance, or war club from an enemy's hands. One such spectacular coup, witnessed by hundreds of warriors, was accomplished by a Pawnee when the Cheyennes moved in force against their Pawnee enemies. Their leader, Bull, was to lead the charge against the Pawnees waiting for the attack a few hundred yards away. The Cheyenne medicine man tied the bundle containing the greatest medicine of the tribe, the four sacred arrows, to Bull's lance and sent him on his way, followed by hundreds of Cheyennes and their allies. One sick Pawnee, wishing to die honorably in battle rather than waste away in his tipi, walked out well in front of his comrades and sat down to await his doom. When Bull charged and struck with his lance, the Pawnee in some manner parried the lance thrust and wrested the weapon from the astounded warrior. Seeing their medicine destroyed in such spectacular fashion, the Cheyennes retreated in disorder leaving the sick man to die slowly but in great honor.

During the nineteenth century the gun was added to the list of weapons, and in at least one tribe the snatching of a shield also counted, but usually the enemy had to be struck down before the shield could be taken from his arm.

Thus it was theoretically possible for a very brave warrior who was exceptionally quick and strong to charge up to an armed enemy, parry his blow, strike him with a coup stick, wrest away his weapon, then kill and scalp him all in one brief encounter, the whole affair lasting no more than a minute or two. If a Dakota warrior accomplished all this he would rate four of the highest coups for his work.

All of these deeds, except scalping, were accomplished in combat. Another high honor could be earned in many tribes by a man who was the leader of a successful raid. If the leader brought all of his men back safely, even though the whole party captured only one or two horses, he received great credit. His medicine was strong; his spirit helpers were with him. But if he lost even one of his men, he was discredited, even though his party returned with several scalps and a whole band of stolen horses.

Among the Crows, for instance, a party that had lost a man was expected to stay away from the camp for ten days, hiding out in the hills close by after sending one man in to tell the bad news. As soon as the omens were right for another raid the same men went seeking the enemy camp. Then if they returned with no more losses and even one captured horse they were received in the camp as victors, but the family of the dead man remained in deep mourning and craved revenge at the earliest opportunity.

Thus it was of paramount importance for any leader to have very strong medicine and to choose an appropriate time for his departure. Usually a vivid dream containing the right omens for success was the initial stimulus for organizing a raiding party. And not always did the dream have to come to the proposed leader. At times a close relative, usually the mother, of the man killed by the enemy had a dream that indicated the time was ripe for the male relatives to seek adequate revenge.

Even though all the signs were right and the war party had set out, some strong, unfavorable omen could send them all home before they reached enemy land. In 1847 the Kiowas were invited by some Comanches to join in a raid on the Utes in the Colorado mountains.[1] Everything seemed favorable and a hundred or more men from the two tribes set out toward the west. The first night out the Comanches killed and ate a bear, an action strictly taboo to the two ranking Kiowas, so they turned back at once with most of their men. The action ended in disaster with all but four of the Kiowas who continued with the Comanches killed in a big fight with the Utes. An interesting item on the size of Kiowa war parties comes from this story. As the party was about to set out from the Kiowa camp one of the men remarked that it was about the greatest war party anybody had ever heard of. He must have meant among the Kiowas for he surely knew of the big battle between the Comanches and Kiowas against the Cheyennes and Arapahoes a few years earlier. After the Kiowa leader had returned he said that there were too many men for good fighting anyway.

Another spectacular failure of apparently strong, favorable medicine failing a large war party came at the second battle of Adobe Walls in 1874.[2] The Comanche medicine man had done his very best, producing a spell that he said would hold the whites at Adobe Walls in deep sleep at the critical time. He also offered to individual warriors at an additional price a bullet-proofing charm for the day of the fight. But on the way to the fight, just a short time before the charge was to be made, one of the Comanche allies killed a skunk. With the medicine ruined by this thoughtless deed the Comanches lost the battle and some of the young men were shot right through their bullet proofing by the buffalo guns in the hands of the defenders.

The northern tribes with as many as ten social groups for the men usually had one dedicated to unusual bravery in battle. Among the Crows and Arapahoes these were called the Crazy Dogs. They were expected to do several kinds of crazy things, such as meaning the direct opposite of what they said. They were always to be in the van of any fighting force and sometimes were under a solemn oath never to retreat in the face of an enemy. Sometimes one of them took an even more demanding oath to deliberately seek death in battle. Each of these vows was considered as fulfilled if the man survived the next fight. In a season when fighting was slack, he was released from his oath by the coming of winter that marked the end of the raiding season.

Among the Crazy Dogs one man of unusual valor was given the added responsibility of carrying a special spear and wearing a sacred sash. When his war party met a dangerous foe and took up a strong defensive position on foot on some knoll or rise of ground, he was obliged to stand at the point of greatest danger. There he allowed one end of his sash to rest on the ground and pinned it down with his spear. If the fighting went against his party, the only way he could be saved from certain death was for one of his own brothers or one of the Crazy Dogs to come to his aid and pull up the spear, thus freeing him to make his retreat.

The Arapahoes to the south of the Crows had such a Crazy Dog society, but it was unknown on the southern Plains until after the peace council at Bent's Fort in 1840. Although the Kiowas had brought the Dog Soldier concept and about five societies south with them when they left the Black Hills in 1805, they did not have the Crazy Dog society until after 1840. This was copied directly from that of the Southern Arapahoes, and indicates that at least one of the Kiowas had a rather close friendship with an Arapaho. This probably stemmed from their boyhood days when the Kiowas, living north of the Black Hills, were neighbors of the Arapahoes just to the southwest. Now after a lapse of thirty-five years these friends met again at the peace council, all of them mature men in their fifties taking part in the affairs of the tribes. This renewal of friendship was made easy because there had never been any real enmity between the Kiowas and the Arapahoes, only between the Comanches and Cheyennes and these two had been drawn in to the conflict as allies of the combatants for just the one big fight.

Horse stealing was a young man's game. Most of those volunteering for the raids were in their late teens or early twenties although the leader might be thirty or more. When the call came, off they went on a lark, their minds filled with visions of glory, of parading before the entire camp in their finery, of being able to give presents of horses to relatives and friends.

A war party setting out on a mission of revenge was a more serious matter and required more planning as well as a more experienced leader with a deserved reputation for success in such enterprises. Usually the war party was larger, and was made up of many hardy, well-tested fighters in their late twenties and early thirties. There are several reported happenings that indicate war parties were always directed against specific enemies who had killed one or more of the tribe and so had incurred blood debts. Often the war parties showed no animosity toward small groups from strange tribes. Otherwise it is difficult to explain how small war parties of Blackfeet who were reported from time to time as raiding the horse herds of the traders along the Santa Fe Trail a thousand miles from Blackfoot territory escaped being hunted down and wiped out by some of the warlike tribes in the area who surely knew the alien raiders were there and from what tribe they came.

Before the Southern Cheyennes moved from the Black Hills to southwestern Kansas, several small bands of Cheyennes were reported over the years along the Santa Fe Trail, yet there is no indication that they suffered attacks from the Kiowas or Comanches until after a time they began to steal Comanche horses. They even were welcomed in a large camp with Indians from several different tribes where a trader was dispensing his wares.[3] However, by 1827 any Cheyenne caught in the valley of the Arkansas River was killed out of hand.

In addition to these incidents, there are several more concerning young men just out to see the world who were allowed safe passage through many different tribes.

Much more was expected of a war party out on the vengeance trail than from those just after horses. The latter could claim a successful venture if they brought back even one horse for the whole group and did not lose any of their men. A war party seeking blood revenge could not claim success for bringing back a hundred captured horses, but was expected to produce evidence, usually a scalp, of at least one enemy killed, for it took enemy blood to wipe out the blood stain of a kinsman. The scalp might be that of an old woman or even a child, but it still counted full value for the blood revenge. In either case a successful group was entitled to some ceremony and rejoicing to mark their return although the horse raiders usually had to be content with the celebrations confined to their immediate families.

If the horse thieves by good luck had lifted a scalp or two along the way they were entitled to full honors, the same elaborate ceremonies that were awarded the successful war party. The whole pattern for the return was all laid out for them by custom and needed careful staging in order that each man might receive all the public recognition that he had earned. The routine began with the group stopping a few miles away from camp and well out of sight to prepare themselves. Among the Crows and some of the other tribes an important part of the advance preparation was the killing of a buffalo bull. Some of the blood was mixed with powdered charcoal, giving a smooth paint for decorating the robes and shirts and the faces of the men. Any man who had killed an enemy, and anyone who had counted first, second, third, or fourth coup on the raid had his face blackened and a black pattern put on his shirt or robe, with less of the shirt or robe being covered for the lower ranking coups. When all this had been done any loot such as weapons, regalia, trappings, and all the captured horses were arranged to show to the best advantage.

When everything was ready the band rode toward the camp and on topping the last rise began shooting off their guns and yelling to attract a great deal of attention. The camp turned out to welcome them with cheers and set to work at once to arrange a series of songs, dances, feasts, and the like that would occupy the next two or three days. A most important part of the homecoming was the large council meeting with all the men of the tribe seated around the campfire and the women and children standing behind them.

After some ceremonial smoking of the pipes each returning warrior stood up and recited his accomplishments on the raid. If he rated an honor for counting coup, snatching a gun, killing a foeman, or stealing a picketed horse, he called on his comrades to testify in his behalf that he had actually done what he claimed. For in the matter of honors, it did not matter how great a deed he had accomplished out by himself, even wresting a weapon from a foeman, then killing and scalping him, he could not claim any public honor even though he had the enemy's gun, scalp, and horse as evidence to support his story. Of course he would be given credit for it all, but he could not receive the formal award.

Some white observers at such tribal ceremonies tended to downgrade these warriors as windy braggarts, but that was far from the case. They were doing nothing more than making a public record of their deeds in the only way recognized in their culture where they had no written records. In modern organized armies some men are detailed after each battle to listen to the detailed reports of the survivors and to make a record of these experiences. In this way the army can determine which men should be decorated for bravery, but in most armies high decorations can be awarded only if the deed has been witnessed by his comrades, and for the highest honors, by a superior officer. Note that the only essential difference between the two procedures is that the Indian gives his account before the whole tribe, while the soldier gives his to two or three men, but he received his publicity for his deed later and often on a large scale, much larger than that of the warrior.

Thus when an Assiniboin warrior gained his honors and later wore them on his ceremonial regalia, such as his war bonnet, or showed them by special paint marks on his face, he was no more out of line than an American soldier wearing his combat ribbons and the like on his dress uniform. Note that an Indian braggart had no chance at all to impress his audience and so win an award for a phony deed, any more than a modern soldier could get the official award of a high decoration on his own invented story.

The list of war honors and the kind of insignia to denote each one varied greatly from tribe to tribe. The Blackfeet, for instance, had a much longer list of war honors than did the Crows or Assiniboins. Seemingly the Blackfeet did not adopt the idea of the coup stick, for no one mentions their use of this object. Their highest rating was given for the wresting of a gun from a foe. Close to this came the taking by force a bow, shield, or war bonnet. These latter two a Crow would mention, but would receive no special credit for them. Below these deeds the Blackfeet ranked the taking of a scalp and, at the bottom of the list but still an honor, the capturing of a horse. Perhaps the great difference in the Crow and Blackfoot rankings on horse stealing can be explained by the fact that the Crows were rated as the cleverest horse thieves on all the Plains, so stealing even a band of horses was rather routine for them and not worth an extra honor. The Blackfeet did not list the taking of a picketed horse, possibly because they seldom accomplished this feat.

Among the Iowas, being a successful war leader on several raids rated the highest honor, while killing an enemy, counting coup, probably on the corpse, and scalping followed in that order.

All of the Plains tribes changed their costumes so rapidly and so drastically in the 1880s under the influence of the many Wild West shows it is difficult to list the sort of markings used in each tribe for each honor won in the earlier days. Among the Assiniboins an eagle feather could be worn for each enemy killed. Some war bonnets made by the various Plains tribes but passed from hand to hand and tribe to tribe by capture or trade have eagle feathers around the crown with many of these feathers carrying one or another of a variety of distinctive marks at the tips. It easily might be that each kind of mark represented some honor or lesser recognition, but there is no way now of determining their exact significance, and often it is difficult to even identify the tribe making the bonnet. This use of eagle feathers was very popular among many of the Dakota nomadic bands and may have been instituted by them. It is quite obvious that the more elaborate war bonnets were designed to be worn by horsemen out in the open country in a formal parade. They would have been entirely out of place in any woodland or rainy environment.

When the significance of these war bonnets and of the individual feathers on each are considered, it is obvious that this insignia of the great fighting men of the Plains has been debased a great deal in the last half a century. Now the great war bonnet, the Indian's highest military decoration, is nothing more than a colorful item of Indian costumes that can be recognized as Indian by almost anyone. It is now worn at almost any place, any time, and by anybody who wants to indicate that the wearer is an Indian or is supposed to be dressed like an Indian. Today many Indians from many tribes whose ancestors had never seen a war bonnet until they began attending Wild West shows claim the war bonnet as a proper distinctive badge of their own tribes.

In the various Plains tribes other decorations besides eagle feathers could be worn to denote various honors. Among the Crows the coup striker sometimes wore the tips of wolves' tails on the heels of his moccasins that were used only for special occasions, while a comrade could show that he had wrested a gun from a foeman by decorating his shirt with ermine skins. A captain successful in several raids could advertise his standing by having his shirt and moccasins trimmed with hair.

In addition to these formal decorations there were hundreds of items that might be used as costume trimming for their novelty, rarity, beauty, or value. Since these items could usually be worn by either men or women and seldom were added in a definite pattern prescribed by the tribe, they serve to confuse the attempts to separate them from the badges denoting formal honors.

18

The Sun Dance

THE HORSE CULTURE COMPLEX of the Plains tribes was almost entirely Spanish and was diffused almost unadulterated along with the horses from the colony in New Mexico. The horse and its accompanying trappings were accepted readily by every one of the Plains tribes with no observable conflict with their varying cultures. As a result all of the mounted Indians of the Plains appeared very much alike to the casual visitor.

Once the hunting of buffalo by large parties of horsemen became common, the supervision of the tribal hunts was so necessary that Dog Soldier societies or their equivalents were accepted in the Plains to control all the people during the hunt, with the controls being more rigid among the seminomadic tribes than among the true nomads. While the basic pattern for these camp police was much the same throughout the Plains, there was a marked difference between the source of authority in the tribes of the Siouan family, where the camp police were always social groups, and tribes of the Caddoan family whose camp police were religious groups, but this difference was not apparent to the casual observer.

In the rules for the war game there was some variation from tribe to tribe, and the list of honors also varied, with the more elaborate structures among the Dakotas and their neighbors in the northeast. It is possible that these were considered to be more elaborate because several detailed studies were made among these tribes and some artists sketched hundreds of scenes along the Missouri River, while such observations and drawings were lacking for the tribes on the southern Plains. Here again the similarities among the various tribes were more apparent than the differences.

The Sun Dance ritual seems to have been spread from tribe to tribe on a pattern different from any of these other culture complexes mentioned above. The division between the tribes staging various versions of the Sun Dance and those other tribes showing no interest in the ritual is sharp and was obvious to the early visitors. The Sun Dance celebrants are all nomadic tribes although they are from varying cultural backgrounds and language groups. The seminomadic tribes with the same backgrounds and from the same language groups definitely met their needs in other ways. This is a strong indication that there was something in the yearly cycle of nomadic life that strongly inclined toward the Sun Dance ritual and the accompanying activities.

Early observers gave this ritual the misleading name of Sun Dance although it is decidedly not a form of sun worship. During the spectacular self-torture ceremony which is a part of all Sun Dances, the participants had to stare at the sun for a long period. This one feature then has given the name Sun Dance to the whole aggregation of activities and ceremonies found in the assemblage of a large number of people all of the same tribe, although at times a few visitors from other tribes were allowed.

Among the nomads almost the entire year was spent with the people scattered about in small bands of possibly two hundred people or fewer in each. Their horse herd would then contain from three hundred to five hundred horses and all of these had to secure their entire food supply by grazing. In any much larger camp the problem of securing ample grass for a thousand or more horses within reasonable distance was formidable, and the difficulty of guarding the herd against enemy raiders increased rapidly as the herd was moved farther away. Even with the smaller herd the people had to move camp every few days so their horses could have fresh pasture.

The nomads preferred their buffalo meat fresh every day which meant that the hunters had to kill a few animals, about ten or so each week. These could be killed in a small hunt by attacking a little band of buffalo feeding on the outskirts of the main herd, often without alarming any of the other bands into taking flight. The herd would then continue to graze in the area for some time. A much larger camp, with so many people to feed, had a much greater problem in killing enough buffalo to feed all their people without alarming the main herd.

Especially in the winter time the camps had to be small and at least a few miles apart so the horses from each camp could find forage and shelter for possibly two months at a time. The camp was placed in a river bottom where the leafless trees and bushes served as windbreaks for the tipis and supplied fuel for the fires. Buffalo chips might serve nicely as fuel for about nine months of the year, but they were difficult to collect in sufficient quantity when the blizzards were blowing and the temperature dropped well below zero for days at a time.

Cottonwood groves were much the best for winter camps in the northern Plains. Both the Crows and Blackfeet liked to cut the trees for logs for their shelters or for firewood. These trees were then stripped of their bark, and this, with the twigs, furnished good forage for the horses when the new snows lay deep on the grassy hills. The old mountain men proved time and again that horses raised on the open range could winter well on nothing more to eat during the storms than the freshly peeled bark from green cottonwood trees and their animals seemed to relish this diet.

After nine or ten months living around the country in small bands, the people were all in the mood for large social gatherings. Early in June, when the new grass was at its best and the young bulls were fat and sleek, was the ideal time for all the bands of one tribe to assemble in one big camp for several days of feasting and frolic. In time they added various ceremonies and finally came to that spectacular drama that culminated in the self-torture of young warriors anxious for public approval, or in search of special spiritual help for their summer's activities on the warpath.

But the seminomadic tribes had no such urge for a large meeting of their people in the early summer. They had been together through the entire winter, with occasional large gatherings for feasting or the winter dances. Then when spring came they had worked around the villages building new homes, repairing old ones, and digging up and planting their farm plots. So when early summer brought the nomadic bands together in large social groups, the seminomadic tribes were scattering their people in small bands throughout the Plains near their villages to enjoy the interval between the spring planting and the fall harvesting of the crops. Their social and ceremonial needs had been satisfied during the winter.

This important difference in the yearly cycles of these two kinds of tribes may explain this sharp divergence in the types of summer activities, a divergence that shows plainly only in this one area of activity.

Although the nomadic Plains tribes vary a great deal in their religious ceremonies and in a multitude of minor items that make up the bulk of their Sun Dance activities, they are remarkably alike in the general overall pattern, having in common such items as the Sun Dance Lodge with its special center pole. It is probable that each tribe had some sort of assemblage for many years, featuring their own tribal ceremonies and later borrowed the general pattern while making very little or no change in their older procedure. The center of distribution for this general pattern has not been identified, but it would appear that one of the tribes established an interesting structure that all the other tribes soon adopted with only minor variations.

In all of these tribes the Sun Dance, like the other societies and religious activities, is concerned with the success of their men in war, and the concept of blood revenge is the motivating force. Even when the Sun Dance is given more as a thank offering for the safe return of a warrior, a favorable ceremony is expected to give the sponsors assistance and protection in future conflicts.

Each tribe had one man in charge of all the Sun Dance activities. The Kiowas called him the Sun Dance priest, while among the Crows he was the camp chief. This man announced to the tribe the name of the person sponsoring the Sun Dance, appointed one of the men's societies to act as camp police for the event, and sent out scouts to select a desirable site for the large encampment.

There was a great deal of ritual connected with every stage of the ceremonies. A mourner who decided that he wanted revenge for one of his dead kinsmen did not go right out and announce his decision to the camp. Instead he would say to the man who was about to cut his hair, "Leave a little hair on my head so I can tie a feather on it." The haircutter knew that such a feather was tied on only by a mourner who was fasting for a Sun Dance so he would tell the camp chief. Or the mourner might ask that all the bulls' tongues be saved at the next hunt and the camp chief would know that they were to be used for a Sun Dance and would make the necessary announcement.

A Sun Dance ceremony was expected to last until the mourner had his vision. If this took several days he might need a thousand or more tongues to feed the people helping him even though these tongues were carefully apportioned among the people only at lunchtime, and presumably represented only a portion of the food they ate at each meal. Since for each tongue a bull in his prime died, the meat from several hundred buffalo was to rot on the prairie because that was more than the whole camp could eat in three months, and not all the meat could be dried when the whole camp was very busy with the ceremonies.

After the Sun Dance was announced, the mourner had to find a man who owned one of the special Doll bundles to take charge of the ceremony. For this service the mourner paid a great deal to the Doll owner who became his "father" for the period of the Sun Dance. Usually this payment covered the purchase of the Doll bundle, too.

As soon as the Sun Dance was scheduled, scouts went out hunting a suitable place. Of course they knew in advance all the possible places within a hundred miles around, but they needed to decide which one was the best at this particular time. They could not choose any site that had been used for a large meeting within the last three or four years, for it took that long for the grass and shrubbery to recover from the trampling of thousands of people and horses. Then, too, if a large herd of buffalo had pastured on the spot lately, there would be no grass for the horses for at least another year.

Once the site had been chosen and the people began to assemble, the camp police laid out the camp and assigned to each band its portion of the great tipi circle. For the Blackfeet the scouts had to find three more campsites nearby, for they never went directly to the main site but approached it in four short marches in as many days. Other tribes usually assembled at the site.

The next great event was the erection of the Sun Lodge. All the tribes agreed that the Lodge needed a very special center pole, a cottonwood with a strong fork near the top. When the scouts reported the finding of the suitable tree, a special group composed of the mourner, his "father," the scouts, and a chaste woman went out to cut down the tree, followed by a large crowd of onlookers and the many people chosen to help bring in the tree, the other posts, many poles for the rafters, and the like.

Although it was considered a very high honor to be chosen as the chaste woman, among the Crows the candidate sometimes refused, for her participation bound her to never remarry if her husband died. If the chosen woman had some shady incident in her past that made her ineligible she would say, "No, I have a hole in my moccasin." In some of the southern tribes the chosen woman had to be a young captive, a practice that may have been borrowed from the Pawnees who did not have a Sun Dance but had a spectacular ceremony dedicated to the Morning Star.

After a great deal of preliminary ceremonies, the tree was cut down by some special person, and was treated as a fallen enemy. The warriors dashed in and counted coup on it as they broke off the limbs with their war clubs and stripped off the bark. Then the log was taken to the lodge site and a number of special articles were tied in a bundle. A bunch of brush was tied in the fork of the tree, the bundle was lashed to it, and in some cases a man chosen to represent a large bird, either the thunderbird or an eagle, according to the tribe, ascended the pole and sat on his nest for a time.

Around the great center post, projecting about thirty feet in the air, a circle of shorter posts were placed with their tops joined by heavy poles lashed into place. Then long rafter poles were placed reaching from the fork of the center pole to the outer circle, and finally the structure was partially covered with leafy branches. Near the base of the center pole a small square was cleared of grass and sod to represent an altar. It was decorated with buffalo skulls.

When the structure was finally completed, all the young men who had vowed in advance to undergo the torture presented themselves. The medicine men made two parallel slits in each breast of each man, with a skewer of smooth wood passed through each pair of slits with the ends protruding. To these ropes were tied, with the other ends tied to the fork of the center pole. Then each young man leaned back, keeping his ropes taut while he alternately raised himself on his toes and sank back, all the while gazing at the sun. He persisted in his dancing until the skewers finally tore loose under his weight and released him. If his ropes still held when evening came, a medicine man might slash the flesh a little to speed the breaking. In one reported case the medicine man threw his weight on the young man's shoulders, forcibly tearing him loose.

Some of the young men had their ropes fastened in like manner to each shoulder blade with one or more buffalo skulls tied to each rope. He dashed around outside the ring of dancers until the jerking of the skulls tore the ropes loose. After this ordeal each participant required several weeks for his wounds to heal and he carried his scars to his grave.

While these and the other ceremonies were in progress the mourner went entirely without food and usually without water. He underwent an elaborate series of purifications day by day. When he finally collapsed from exhaustion he was revived and was expected to give an account of the visions he had been seeking.

Among the Blackfeet the sponsor of the Sun Dance was a woman who had taken a vow to stage the dance if a dear one came back safely from a war party or recovered from a grievous wound or a severe illness. In an ordinary year there would be several who had made their vows. They then joined their efforts, but each was required to buy one of the sacred bundles at a high price. They then secured help from several of their friends and under the direction of an experienced Sun Dance director, made all the preparations and helped erect the lodge. They too needed a very large number of buffalo tongues. Unlike the Crow mourner, these women did not expect to receive visions.

The Blackfeet added a nice touch to insure good weather. They had two or more men who danced at frequent intervals all day long during the four days of preparation to keep the rain away. No mention was made of what happened to the dancers if it did rain there in a land where showers in the early summer are quite the common thing.

The Sun Dance continued to spread among the Plains tribes until in 1874 the Comanches finally adopted a modified version. During the period of great turmoil on the Plains when the buffalo were slaughtered and tribes fought so many losing battles against the soldiers before they were finally penned on their reservations, many of the old rituals often had to be postponed. Then a new religious movement, started in southwestern Nevada by the Paviotso messiah, Wovoka, swept through the Plains. It rapidly culminated in the Ghost Dance, but collapsed completely after the disaster at Wounded Knee.

The Sun Dance, along with several other Indian ceremonies, was in disfavor with the Indian Bureau officials. It was banned entirely in 1904, but was reinstated in 1935. Over the years when it was not staged, many of the older people who remembered the rituals died. The new version is a drastic revision of the old and the tribes that want to revive the old ceremonies are forced to turn to the white man's records in ethnological studies for the details that have long been forgotten by the tribesmen.

Notes

Chapter 1

1. Louis A. Brennan, *No Stone Unturned*, p. 101.

Chapter 2

1. Herbert E. Bolton, *Coronado: Knight of the Pueblos and Plains*, p. 146.
2. James H. Gunnerson, *The Fremont Culture*, p. 17 ff.

Chapter 5

1. George E. Hyde, *Indians of the High Plains*, p. 47n.
2. Washington Irving, *Adventures of Captain Bonneville*, p. 171.
3. Ibid., p. 70.

Chapter 6

1. F. V. Scholes, "Troublous Times in New Mexico, 1659–1670," *New Mexico Historical Review*, Vol. 12, p. 142.
2. Hyde, p. 37.
3. Ibid., p. 67.
4. Ibid., 80 ff.
5. Rupert Norval Richardson, *The Comanche Barrier to South Plains Settlement*, p. 67.
6. Hyde, p. 162.
7. Ibid.

Chapter 9

1. David Thompson, *David Thompson's Narrative of His Explorations in Western America, 1784–1812*, p. 336 ff.

Chapter 10

1. Lewis Hector Girrard, *Wah-to-yah and the Taos Trail*, p. 73.

Chapter 11

1. Hyde, p. 20.
2. Thompson, p. 338.
3. Ibid., p. 370.
4. John C. Ewers, *The Blackfeet*, p. 47.
5. David Lavender, *Bent's Fort*, p. 132 ff.

Chapter 12

1. Bernard De Voto, *Across the Wide Missouri*, p. 279 ff.

Chapter 13

1. Le Roy Hafen and Ann W. Hafen, eds. *To the Rockies and Oregon, 1839–1842*, p. 223.
2. Allen Nevins, ed. *Narratives of Explorations*, p. 60.
3. Charles J. Kappler, ed. *Indian Affairs, Laws and Treaties*, Vol. 2, p. 594.

Chapter 16

1. Robert H. Lowie, *The Crow Indians*, p. 5.
2. Louis Hennepin, *A New Discovery of a Vast Country in America*, Vol. I, p. 158.
3. Thompson, p. 370.

Chapter 17

1. Alice Marriott, *The Ten Grandmothers*, p. 11 ff.
2. Francis Haines, *The Buffalo*, p. 198.
3. Donald J. Berthrong, *The Southern Cheyennes*, p. 21.

Selected Bibliography

THE BASIC DATA on all the tribes was taken from John R. Swanton, *The Indian Tribes of North America*, Bureau of American Ethnology Bulletin 145, 1953, Washington, D.C. Supplementary material came from Robert H. Lowie, *Indians of the Plains*, New York, 1954, and two works by George E. Hyde, *Indians of the High Plains* and *Indians of the Woodlands*, Norman, Oklahoma, 1959 and 1962. Some material was used from each of the following:

Berthrong, Donald J. *The Southern Cheyennes*, Norman, Oklahoma: University of Oklahoma Press, 1963.

Bolton, Herbert E. *Coronado: Knight of the Pueblos and Plains*, Albuquerque, New Mexico: University of New Mexico Press, 1949.

Brennan, Louis A. *No Stone Unturned*, New York, New York: Random House, 1959.

De Voto, Bernard. *Across the Wide Missouri*, Boston, Massachusetts: Houghton Mifflin Co., 1947.

Ewers, John C. *The Blackfeet*, Norman, Oklahoma: University of Oklahoma Press, 1958.

Girrard, Lewis Hector. *Wah-to-yah and the Taos Trail* (ed. by Ralph P. Beiber), Glendale, California: Arthur H. Clarke Co., 1938.

Gunnerson, James H. *The Fremont Culture, a study in culture dynamics on the northern Anasazi frontier. Including the report of Clafin-Emerson expedition of the Peabody Museum*, Cambridge, Massachusetts: Peabody House, 1969.

Hafen, Le Roy, and Hafen, Ann W., eds. *To the Rockies and Oregon, 1839–1842*, Glendale, Calif., Arthur H. Clark & Co. 1955.

Hennepin, Louis. *A New Discovery of a Vast Country in America* (Reprinted from the Second London Issue of 1968), 2 vols., Chicago, Illinois: A. C. McClurg Co., 1903.

Irving, Washington. *Adventures of Captain Bonneville*, New York: Thomas Y. Crowell, 1843.

Kappler, Charles J., ed. *Indian Affairs, Laws and Treaties*, 4 vols., 1904–1909, Washington, D.C.: AMS Press, Inc.

Lavender, David. *Bent's Fort*, New York, New York: Peter Smith, 1954.

Lowie, Robert H. *The Crow Indians*, New York, New York: Holt, Rinehart and Winston, Inc., 1935.

Marriott, Alice. *The Ten Grandmothers*, Norman, Oklahoma: University of Oklahoma Press, 1945.

Nevins, Allen, ed. *Narratives of Explorations and Adventures of John Charles Fremont*, New York, Longmans, Green Co. 1956.

Parkman, Francis. *The Oregon Trail*, New York: Holt, Rinehart and Winston, Inc., 1931.

Richardson, Rupert Norval. *The Comanche Barrier to South Plains Settlement*, Glendale, California: Kraus Reprint, Co., 1933.

Scholes, F. V. "Troublous Times in New Mexico, 1659–1670," *New Mexico Historical Review*, Vol. 12, pp. 134–74, 1937.

Thompson, David. *David Thompson's Narrative of His Explorations in Western America, 1784–1812*, ed. by J. B. Tyrell, Toronto, Ontario: Greenwood, 1916.

For additional reading in this field there is a wealth of material in the *Civilization of the American Indian Series*, University of Oklahoma Press, Norman, Oklahoma.

Index